Acorn Cottage

Quilts with Simple & Sophisticated Style

BRENDA RIDDLE

Martingale®
Create with Confidence

Acorn Cottage: Quilts with Simple & Sophisticated Style
© 2020 by Brenda Riddle

Martingale®
19021 120th Ave. NE, Ste. 102
Bothell, WA 98011-9511 USA
ShopMartingale.com

Printed in China
25 24 23 22 21 20   8 7 6 5 4 3 2 1

Library of Congress Cataloging-in-Publication Data is available upon request.

ISBN: 978-1-68356-057-9

MISSION STATEMENT

We empower makers who use fabric and yarn to make life more enjoyable.

CREDITS

PUBLISHER AND CHIEF VISIONARY OFFICER
Jennifer Erbe Keltner

CONTENT DIRECTOR
Karen Costello Soltys

MANAGING EDITOR
Tina Cook

ACQUISITIONS AND DEVELOPMENT EDITOR
Laurie Baker

TECHNICAL EDITOR
Elizabeth Beese

COPY EDITOR
Sheila Chapman Ryan

DESIGN MANAGER
Adrienne Smitke

PRODUCTION MANAGER
Regina Girard

PHOTOGRAPHER
Brent Kane

ILLUSTRATOR
Christine Erikson

SPECIAL THANKS
Photography for this book was taken at the home of Tracie Fish of Bothell, Washington (Instagram: @fishtailcottage), and at Laurie Clark's The Farmhouse Cottage in Snohomish, Washington.

Contents

Introduction

However we were first drawn to quilting, we all share the love of what happens when we put fabric and thread together: a seemingly magical transformation of pieces of fabric (sometimes lots of them!) into a finished quilt that somehow holds a little piece of our heart.

My first memories of quilts are of the ones made by my grandmas, Floye and Estella. The quilts were kept on the upper shelves in the linen closet. My mom knew they were treasures, and I think that's part of why the designs my grandmas made are still so special to me. When the quilts came down off the shelves, it was an important occasion, and they made their way into my heart.

It's also meaningful to me that I share the tradition of quilting with my grandmas. They're with me in a very special way with every quilt I design and every quilt I make.

My favorite quilts reflect those I remember from the linen closet. There's a softness about them, with light and airy backgrounds that bring a cozy cottage feel to wherever they find their home. As you choose which quilt you might make, either for yourself or as a gift for someone special, I hope you find joy in every step of this amazing, magical process.

~Brenda

Tulip Crosses

When I first saw the quilts in the American Folk Art Museum's "Infinite Variety: Red and White Quilts" exhibition, I was amazed by them (and I still am!). Their simplicity, their elegance, and their classic designs captured my heart. One of my favorites, Tulip Crosses, is the inspiration for this quilt.

QUILT SIZE: 86⅞" × 86⅞"
BLOCK SIZE: 12½" × 12½"

MATERIALS

Yardage is based on 42"-wide fabric. Fat eighths measure 9" × 21".

- 25 fat eighths of assorted pink, green, tan, and aqua prints for blocks
- 7 yards of off-white solid for blocks, sashing, setting triangles, and border
- ⅞ yard of aqua stripe for binding
- 8 yards of fabric for backing
- 95" × 95" square of batting

CUTTING

All measurements include ¼" seam allowances.

From *each* assorted print fat eighth, refer to the diagram below to cut:
4 rectangles, 3" × 5½" (100 total)
2 squares, 3½" × 3½" (50 total)
4 squares, 3" × 3" (100 total)

From the off-white solid, cut:
3 strips, 21¼" × 42"; crosscut into:
   3 squares, 21¼" × 21¼"; cut the squares into quarters diagonally to make 12 setting triangles
   2 squares, 10" × 10"; cut the squares in half diagonally to make 4 corner triangles
2 strips, 8" × 42"; crosscut into 25 rectangles, 3" × 8"
8 strips, 5¼" × 42"
5 strips, 3½" × 42"; crosscut into 50 squares, 3½" × 3½"
20 strips, 3" × 42"; crosscut into 250 squares, 3" × 3"
13 strips, 2" × 42"; crosscut 7 of the strips into 20 rectangles, 2" × 13"

From the aqua stripe, cut:
10 strips, 2½" × 42"

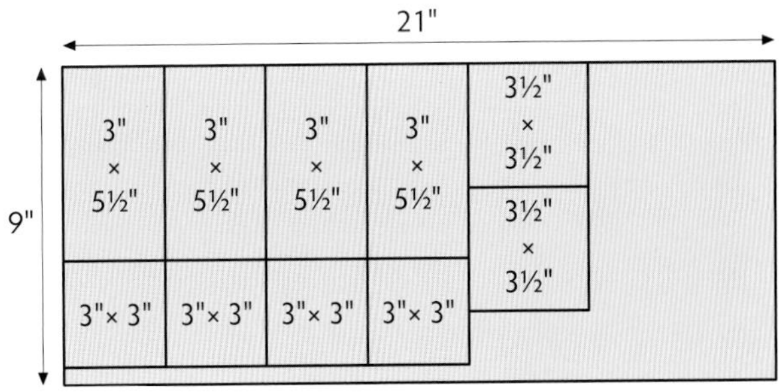

Cutting for fat eighths

Designed and pieced by Brenda Riddle; quilted by Nicole Christoffersen

MAKING THE BLOCKS

Press all seam allowances as indicated by the arrows. Use matching pieces from one of the prints in steps 2–7.

1. Draw a diagonal line on the wrong side of each off-white 3½" square and 100 of the off-white 3" squares.

2. Place a marked off-white 3½" square on top of a print 3½" square with right sides together. Sew ¼" from each side of the drawn line. Cut along the drawn line and press. (You can also press the seam allowances open.) Trim each half-square-triangle unit to 3" square, including seam allowances. Repeat to make four matching half-square-triangle units.

Make 4 units.

3. Place a marked off-white 3" square on one end of a print 3" × 5½" rectangle as shown. Sew on the drawn diagonal line. Trim the corner ¼" from the seam and press. The unit should measure 3" × 5½", including seam allowances. Repeat to make four matching rectangle units.

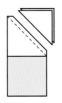

Make 4 units,
3" × 5½".

4. To assemble a corner unit, sew together one half-square-triangle unit, one rectangle unit, and one off-white 3" square as shown. The unit should measure 5½" square, including seam allowances. Repeat to make four matching corner units.

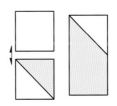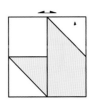

Make 4 units,
5½" × 5½".

5. To make a side unit, sew together one print 3" square and one off-white 3" square. The unit should measure 3" × 5½", including seam allowances. Repeat to make two matching side units.

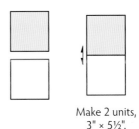

Make 2 units,
3" × 5½".

6. To make the center unit, sew a print 3" square to each end of an off-white 3" × 8" rectangle. The unit should measure 3" × 13", including seam allowances.

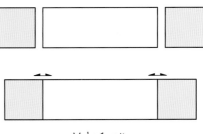

Make 1 unit,
3" × 13".

ASSEMBLING THE QUILT CENTER

1. Sew the six off-white 2" × 42" strips together end to end to make one long strip. From this strip, cut two 69"-long sashing strips and two 41"-long sashing strips.

2. Sew together seven blocks and six off-white 2" × 13" sashing strips to make the center row.

Make 1 row, 13" × 97".

3. Sew together five blocks and four off-white 2" × 13" sashing strips to make a five-block row. Add a 2" × 69" sashing strip to one long edge of the row. Sew setting triangles to each end of the five-block row. Repeat to make two rows.

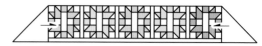

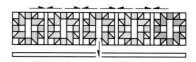

Make 2 rows.

4. Sew together three blocks and two off-white 2" × 13" sashing strips to make a three-block row. Add a 2" × 41" sashing strip to one long edge of the row. Sew setting triangles to each end of the three-block row. Repeat to make two rows.

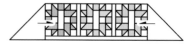

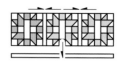

Make 2 rows.

7. To assemble a Tulip Cross block, lay out four corner units, two side units, and one center unit in three rows as shown. Join the rows to make a block, which should measure 13" square, including seam allowances. Repeat steps 2–7 to make 25 Tulip Cross blocks total.

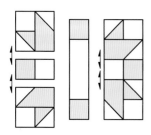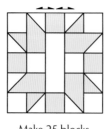

Make 25 blocks, 13" × 13".

5. Sew an off-white 2" × 13" sashing strip to a remaining block. Sew setting triangles to opposite edges of the block to make a one-block row. Repeat to make two rows.

Make 2 rows.

6. Lay out and join the rows as shown in the assembly diagram below. Add the corner triangles. The quilt center should measure 77⅜" square, including seam allowances.

Making On-Point Easy

When joining rows in an on-point quilt, I start by making sure the center blocks and sashing in each row are lined up and centered and then pin outward to each side.

ADDING THE BORDER

Trim the selvages off the eight off-white 5¼" × 42" strips and sew them together end to end. From this long strip, cut two lengths, 77⅜", and two lengths, 86⅞". Sew the 77⅜" lengths to opposite sides of the quilt center. Sew the 86⅞" lengths to the top and bottom edges. Press the seam allowances toward the borders.

FINISHING THE QUILT

For more details on any finishing steps, visit ShopMartingale.com/HowtoQuilt for free, downloadable information.

1. Layer the backing, batting, and quilt top; baste the layers together.

2. Quilt by hand or machine. The quilt shown is machine quilted with an allover leaf design.

3. Use the aqua stripe 2½"-wide strips to make binding, and then attach the binding to the quilt.

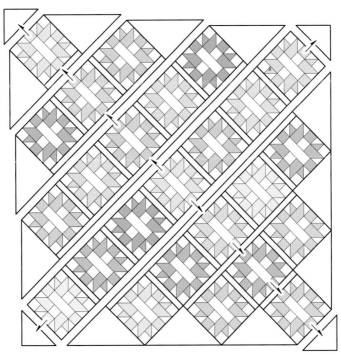

Quilt assembly

Estella

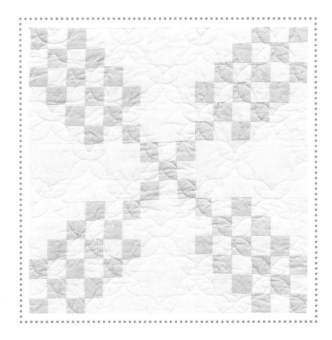

I couldn't resist creating a classic patchwork pattern based on a vintage quilt that stole my heart. Delicate in feel, Estella is named in honor of my maternal grandmother, who was a quilter and whose quilts also captured my heart and nourished a love of quiltmaking.

QUILT SIZE: 57½" × 57½"
BLOCK SIZE: 15" × 15"

MATERIALS

Yardage is based on 42"-wide fabric.

- 1¼ yards of aqua tone on tone for blocks and sashing units
- 3¼ yards of white solid for background and sashing
- ⅝ yard of aqua stripe for binding
- 3¾ yards of fabric for backing
- 64" × 64" piece of batting

CUTTING

From the aqua tone on tone, cut:
26 strips, 1½" × 42"

From the white solid, cut:
2 strips, 15½" × 42"; crosscut into 22 strips, 3½" × 15½"
7 strips, 3½" × 42"; crosscut into:
    2 strips, 3½" × 15½"
    36 rectangles, 3½" × 6½"
5 strips, 2½" × 42"; crosscut into 72 squares, 2½" × 2½"
25 strips, 1½" × 42"

From the aqua stripe, cut:
7 strips, 2½" × 42"

Designed and pieced by Brenda Riddle; quilted by Nicole Christoffersen

MAKING THE BLOCKS

1. To make strip set A, join two aqua and two white 1½" × 42" strips side by side along their long edges. Press. Repeat to make six of strip set A and from these sets, cut 144 A segments, 1½" wide.

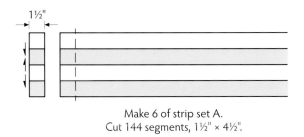

Make 6 of strip set A.
Cut 144 segments, 1½" × 4½".

2. To make strip set B, join three aqua and three white strips side by side along their long edges; press. Repeat to make a total of three of strip set B and crosscut into 72 B segments, 1½" wide.

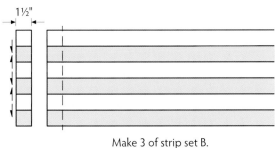

Make 3 of strip set B.
Cut 72 segments, 1½" × 6½".

3. Join the A segments in pairs, rotating one unit so that aqua and white squares are opposite one another in a checkerboard effect. Make 72 A units. Sew a white 2½" square to the bottom of each unit. Units should be 2½" × 6½", including seam allowances.

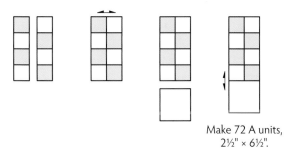

Make 72 A units,
2½" × 6½".

4. Join the B segments in pairs, again rotating one unit so that aqua and white squares are opposite one another. Make 36 B units, 2½" × 6½", including seam allowances.

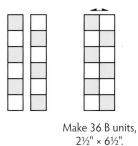

Make 36 B units,
2½" × 6½".

5. To make one block quadrant, sew an A unit to each side of a B unit, rotating them so the larger white squares are at the top right and bottom left, as shown. Make 36. Each quadrant should measure 6½" square, including seam allowances.

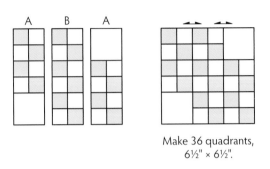

Make 36 quadrants,
6½" × 6½".

6. To make the Nine Patch block centers, join one white and two aqua 1½" × 42" strips to make strip set C. Make two of these strip sets measuring 3½" × 42". Crosscut into 50 C segments, 1½" wide.

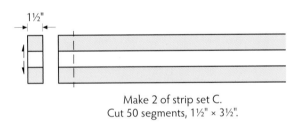

Make 2 of strip set C.
Cut 50 segments, 1½" × 3½".

7. Join one aqua and two white 1½" × 42" strips to make strip set D; press. Crosscut into 25 D segments, 1½" wide.

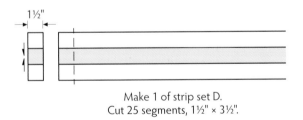

Make 1 of strip set D.
Cut 25 segments, 1½" × 3½".

8. Join two C segments and one D segment to make a nine-patch unit that measures 3½" square. Make 25 units. Nine are for the blocks; set aside the remaining units for the sashing.

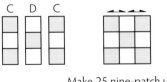

Make 25 nine-patch units,
3½" × 3½".

9. Lay out four block quadrants, four white 3½" × 6½" rectangles, and one nine-patch unit. Join the pieces in rows and then sew the rows together. Press. Repeat to make a total of nine blocks, 15½" square, including seam allowances.

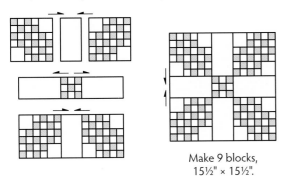

Make 9 blocks,
15½" × 15½".

ASSEMBLING THE QUILT TOP

1. Lay out the nine Estella blocks in three rows of three blocks each. Place a white 3½" × 15½" sashing strip between the blocks and on the outer ends of the block rows.

2. Lay out the sashing rows using the remaining nine-patch units and white 3½" × 15½" strips.

3. Join the pieces in each row, pressing all seam allowances toward the sashing strips. Then join the rows to complete the quilt top, which should measure 57½" square.

FINISHING THE QUILT

For more details on any finishing steps, visit ShopMartingale.com/HowtoQuilt for free downloadable information.

1. Layer the backing, batting, and quilt top; baste the layers together.

2. Quilt by hand or machine. The quilt shown is machine quilted with an allover orange peel design.

3. Use the aqua stripe 2½"-wide strips to make binding, and then attach the binding to the quilt.

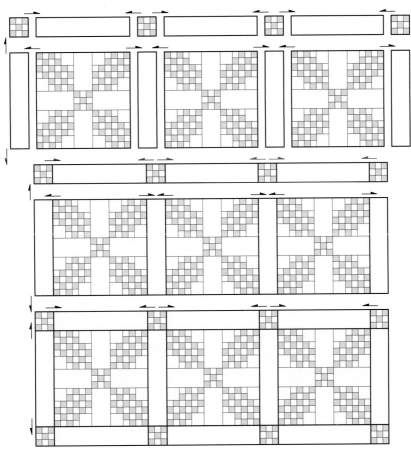

Quilt assembly

Pebbles

imple. Classic. Vintage inspired. These are my favorite elements in the quilts I love. Pebbles has a classic checkerboard pattern that calls out for a good snuggle. I decided to use beautiful warm grays, porcelain whites, and a touch of the softest pinks to create a quilt that would work in different settings.

QUILT SIZE: 60½" × 60½"
BLOCK SIZE: 12" × 12"

MATERIALS

Yardage is based on 42"-wide fabric.

- 1 yard of white-and-gray polka dot for blocks
- 1⅛ yards of ivory print A for blocks
- ¾ yard of ivory print B for blocks
- ⅝ yard of ivory print C for blocks
- ¾ yard of gray print A for blocks
- ⅝ yard of gray print B for blocks
- ⅝ yard of gray print C for blocks
- ¾ yard of pink dot for blocks
- ⅝ yard of ivory floral for binding
- 3¾ yards of fabric for backing
- 67" × 67" square of batting

CUTTING

All measurements include ¼" seam allowances.

From the white-and-gray polka dot, cut:
12 strips, 2½" × 42"; crosscut into 24 strips, 2½" × 21"

From ivory print A, cut:
14 strips, 2½" × 42"; crosscut into 27 strips, 2½" × 21"

From *each* of ivory print B, gray print A, and the pink dot, cut:
9 strips, 2½" × 42"; crosscut into 18 strips, 2½" × 21" (54 total)

From *each* of ivory print C, gray print B, and gray print C, cut:
8 strips, 2½" × 42"; crosscut into 15 strips, 2½" × 21" (45 total)

From the ivory floral, cut:
7 strips, 2½" × 42"

MAKING THE BLOCKS

Press all seam allowances as indicated by the arrows.

1. For each block, choose two colors to pair together from the ivory, gray, white-and-gray, and pink dot fabrics. Using your chosen fabrics, lay out three matching 2½" × 21" strips and three different 2½" × 21" strips, alternating them. Sew the strips together and press the seam allowances toward the darker fabric. Repeat to make 25 strip sets.

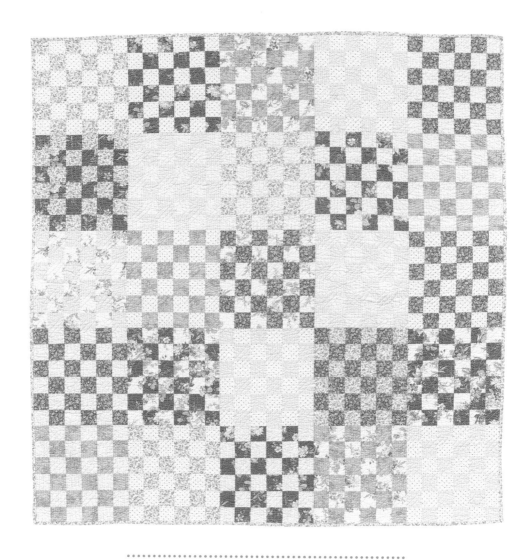

Designed and pieced by Brenda Riddle; quilted by Nicole Christoffersen

2. From each strip set, cut six segments, 2½" wide.

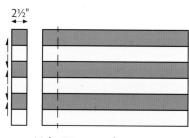

Make 25 assorted strip sets.
Cut 6 segments, 2½" × 12½", from each.

3. Lay out six matching segments, reversing every other one as shown. Sew the strips together to make a Checkerboard block that's 12½" square, including seam allowances. Repeat to make 25 Checkerboard blocks.

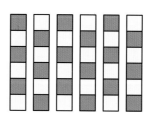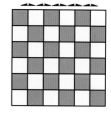

Make 25 blocks,
12½" × 12½".

ASSEMBLING THE QUILT

Lay out the blocks in five rows of five blocks each, arranging them in a way that's pleasing to you. Sew them into rows, and then join the rows to make the quilt top.

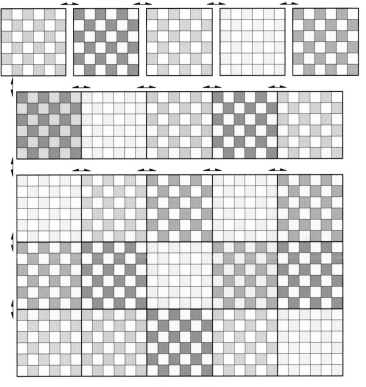

Quilt assembly

FINISHING THE QUILT

For more details on any finishing steps, you can visit ShopMartingale.com/HowtoQuilt for free, downloadable information.

1. Layer the backing, batting, and quilt top; baste the layers together.

2. Quilt by hand or machine. The quilt shown is machine quilted with an allover cable design.

3. Use the ivory floral 2½"-wide strips to make binding, and then attach the binding to the quilt.

Morning Star

I wanted to make my own version of this classic gingham star pattern, which was inspired by a vintage quilt. I simplified the sewing from the original so that you can make it with simple half-square-triangle units and no Y seams!

QUILT SIZE: 68½" × 68½"

MATERIALS

Yardage is based on 42"-wide fabric.

- 1 yard of dark pink print for center star and middle border
- 1⅛ yards of medium pink floral for center star and middle border
- 4⅛ yards of off-white gingham for background and borders
- ⅝ yard of pink gingham for binding
- 4¼ yards of fabric for backing
- 75" × 75" square of batting

CUTTING

All measurements include ¼" seam allowances.

From the dark pink print, cut:
8 strips, 3" × 42"; crosscut into 96 squares, 3" × 3". Cut *24 squares* in half diagonally to make 48 triangles.
2 strips, 2½" × 42"; crosscut into 28 squares, 2½" × 2½"

From the medium pink floral, cut:
11 strips, 3" × 42"; crosscut into 136 squares, 3" × 3". Cut *16 squares* in half diagonally to make 32 triangles.
2 strips, 2½" × 42"; crosscut into 28 squares, 2½" × 2½"

From the off-white gingham, cut:
2 strips, 15½" × 42"; crosscut into 4 squares, 15½" × 15½". Cut each square in half diagonally to make 8 large setting triangles.
2 strips, 11" × 42"; crosscut into 4 squares, 11" × 11". Cut each square in half diagonally to make 8 small setting triangles.
7 strips, 5½" × 42"
6 strips, 3½" × 42"
4 strips, 3" × 42"; crosscut into 48 squares, 3" × 3"
4 strips, 2½" × 42"; crosscut into 56 squares, 2½" × 2½"

From the pink gingham, cut:
8 strips, 2½" × 42"

Designed and pieced by Brenda Riddle; quilted by Bob Jensen

MAKING THE HALF-SQUARE-TRIANGLE UNITS

Press all seam allowances as indicated by the arrows.

1. Draw a diagonal line on the back of a medium pink 3" square. Layer the square with a dark pink 3" square, right sides together. Sew ¼" from each side of the drawn line. Cut along the drawn line and press to make two half-square-triangle units. Trim each unit to measure 2½" square, including seam allowances. Repeat to make 144 medium/dark half-square-triangle units.

2½"
2½"

Make 144 units.

2. Using off-white and medium pink 3" squares, repeat step 1 to make 96 light/medium half-square-triangle units.

Make 96 units,
2½" × 2½".

MAKING THE STAR SECTIONS AND QUILT CENTER

Each quarter of the star has two star points. I think of them as the left-side point (section A) and the right-side point (section B). You will need to make four of each section.

1. To make section A, lay out six dark pink triangles, 18 medium/dark half-square-triangle units, four medium pink triangles, and 12 light/medium half-square-triangle units in five vertical rows as shown. Join the pieces in each row. Sew the rows together. Make four of section A. *Handle these sections carefully since two of the edges are on the bias and can easily stretch out of shape.*

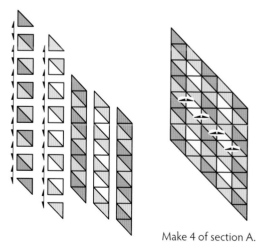

Make 4 of section A.

2. To make section B, repeat step 1, laying out the units in a mirror image of section A as shown. Make four of section B.

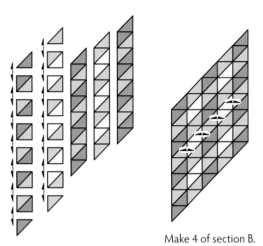

Make 4 of section B.

3. Sew the long sides of small off-white triangles to the top angled edges of an A and a B section as shown; press. Then sew a short edge of a large off-white triangle to the left side of each A section and the right side of each B section.

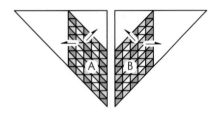

4. Pin and sew together one A and one B section as shown, carefully matching the seams. Make four star-point quarter sections.

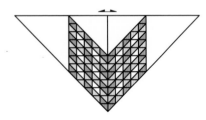

Make 4 star-point quarter sections.

5. Join two star-point quarter sections to make a star-point half section. Make two. Join the half sections to make the quilt center. The quilt center should measure 48½" square, including seam allowances.

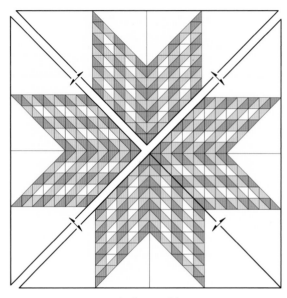

Quilt assembly

ADDING THE BORDERS

1. Trim the selvages off the six off-white 3½" × 42" strips and sew them together end to end. From this long strip, cut two lengths, 48½", and two lengths, 54½". Sew the 48½" lengths to opposite sides of the quilt center. Sew the 54½" lengths to the top and bottom edges.

2. To make a pieced middle border, sew together 14 off-white 2½" squares, seven medium pink 2½" squares, and six dark pink 2½" squares as shown, alternating the squares. Make four pieced middle-border strips.

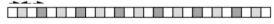

Make 4 middle borders, 2½" × 54½".

3. Sew middle-border strips to opposite sides of the quilt center.

4. Sew a dark pink 2½" square to each end of the remaining middle-border strips. Sew these strips to the top and bottom of the quilt center.

5. Trim the selvages off the seven off-white 5½" × 42" strips and sew them together end to end. From this long strip, cut two lengths, 58½", and two lengths, 68½". Sew the 58½" lengths to opposite sides of the quilt center. Sew the 68½" lengths to the top and bottom edges.

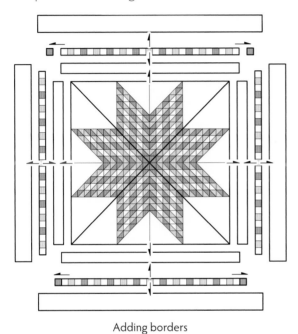

Adding borders

FINISHING THE QUILT

For more details on any finishing steps, visit ShopMartingale.com/HowtoQuilt for free, downloadable information.

1. Layer the backing, batting, and quilt top; baste the layers together.

2. Quilt by hand or machine. The quilt shown is machine quilted with an allover feather design.

3. Use the pink gingham 2½"-wide strips to make binding, and then attach the binding to the quilt.

Hopscotch

Enjoy a classic quilt design with two setting options—straight set (page 33) or on point, as shown here. There are separate directions for each setting. Choose your favorite, or make both for a delightful pair. Follow these directions to set the blocks on point.

QUILT SIZE: 72" × 84"
BLOCK SIZE: 8½" × 8½"

MATERIALS

Yardage is based on 42"-wide fabric.

- 30 squares, 10" × 10", of assorted prints for blocks*
- 1¼ yards of white print A for background of A blocks
- 1 yard of white print B for background of B blocks
- 2⅞ yards of blue floral for setting triangles and border
- ¾ yard of pink gingham for binding
- 5⅛ yards of fabric for backing**
- 80" × 92" piece of batting

*A Moda Layer Cake works well.

**Or 2⅝ yards of 80"-wide fabric.

CUTTING

All measurements include ¼" seam allowances. Each 10" square will provide the print sections needed for one each of blocks A and B. You'll have extra print 2½"×5" rectangles (because there are more of block A than block B). Use the extras to make a backing accent, or cut them up to make a fun set of 2½"-square mini-charms.

From *each* 10" square, refer to the diagram below to cut:
1 square, 5" × 5" (30 total)
4 rectangles, 2½" × 5" (120 total; 40 are extra)
4 squares, 2½" × 2½" (120 total)

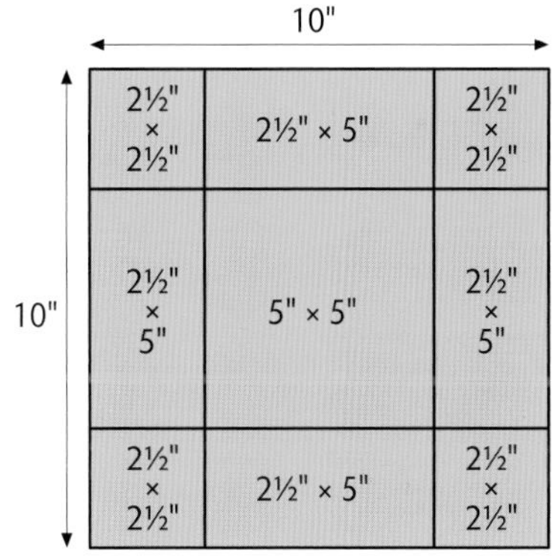

Cutting diagram

From white print A, cut:
8 strips, 5" × 42"; crosscut into 120 rectangles, 2½" × 5"

From white print B, cut:
3 strips, 5" × 42"; crosscut into 20 squares, 5" × 5"
6 strips, 2½" × 42"; crosscut into 80 squares, 2½" × 2½"

Continued on page 30

Continued from page 29

From the blue floral, cut:

2 strips, 13½" × 42"; crosscut into:*
    5 squares, 13½" × 13½"; cut each square into
        quarters diagonally to make 20 setting
        triangles (2 are extra)
    2 squares, 7" × 7"; cut each square in half
        diagonally to make 4 corner triangles
8 strips, 6¼" × 42"

From the pink gingham, cut:

9 strips, 2½" × 42"

*If you're not able to cut all your pieces from two strips, you'll have enough fabric to cut an additional strip.

MAKING THE BLOCKS

Press all seam allowances as indicated by the arrows.

1. Join four white A 2½" × 5" rectangles, four matching print 2½" squares, and one print 5" square in three rows as shown; the 5" square should match the small squares. Join the rows to make block A. The block should measure 9" square, including seam allowances. Repeat to make 30 of block A.

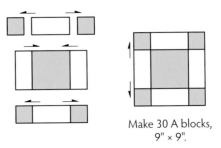

Make 30 A blocks,
9" × 9".

2. Join four matching print 2½" × 5" rectangles, four white B 2½" squares, and one white B 5" square in three rows as shown. Join the rows to make block B. The block should measure 9" square, including seam allowances. Repeat to make 20 of block B.

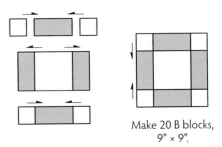

Make 20 B blocks,
9" × 9".

ASSEMBLING THE QUILT TOP

Alternating blocks A and B, lay out the blocks and blue floral setting triangles in 10 diagonal rows. The first and last blocks in each row should be A blocks. Join the blocks in each row, making sure to line up the block seams, and press. Join the rows. Add the blue floral corner triangles to each corner to make the quilt center, which should measure 60½" × 72½", including seam allowances.

ADDING THE BORDER

Trim the selvages off the eight blue floral 6¼" × 42" strips and sew them together end to end. From this long strip, cut two lengths, 72½", and two lengths, 72". Sew the 72½" lengths to opposite sides of the quilt center. Sew the 72" lengths to the top and bottom edges to complete the quilt top. Press the seam allowances toward the border.

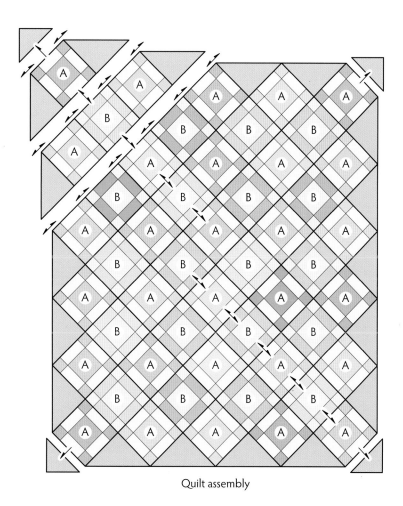

Quilt assembly

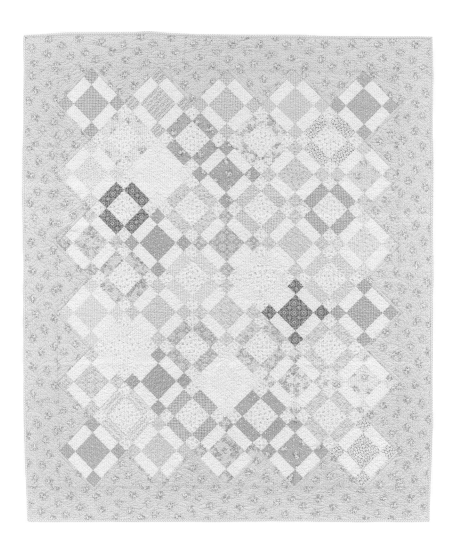

Designed and pieced by Brenda Riddle; quilted by Karolyn "Nubin" Jensen

Add Some Stability

When working with squares that will be cut on the diagonal and used for setting blocks on point, I spray the fabric with sizing or fabric starch before cutting. This helps the triangles better hold their shape (as at least one edge is on the bias).

FINISHING THE QUILT

For more details on any finishing steps, visit ShopMartingale.com/HowtoQuilt for free, downloadable information.

1. Layer the backing, batting, and quilt top; baste the layers together.

2. Quilt by hand or machine. The quilt shown is machine quilted with an allover feather design. The side setting triangles and border allow for some wonderful custom quilting if you wish.

3. Use the pink gingham 2½"-wide strips to make binding, and then attach the binding to the quilt.

Hopscotch 2

Follow these directions to set the blocks in a straight setting. There's just something lovable about a miniature version of a quilt. You can use a mini-quilt in places where a larger version just won't do—on a tabletop, as artwork on a wall, or as a baby quilt. They are perfectly small and perfectly wonderful!

QUILT SIZE: 30" × 37"
BLOCK SIZE: 3½" × 3½"

MATERIALS

Yardage is based on 42"-wide fabric.

- 32 squares, 5" × 5", of assorted prints for blocks*
- ⅜ yard of white print A for background of A blocks
- ⅓ yard of white print B for background of B blocks
- ⅜ yard of green floral for border
- ⅓ yard of pink gingham for binding
- 1 yard of fabric for backing
- 34" × 41" piece of batting

A charm pack works well.

CUTTING

All measurements include ¼" seam allowances.

From *each* 5" square, refer to the diagram below to cut:
1 square, 2½" × 2½" (32 total)
4 rectangles, 1¼" × 2½" (128 total; 4 are extra)
4 squares, 1¼" × 1¼" (128 total)

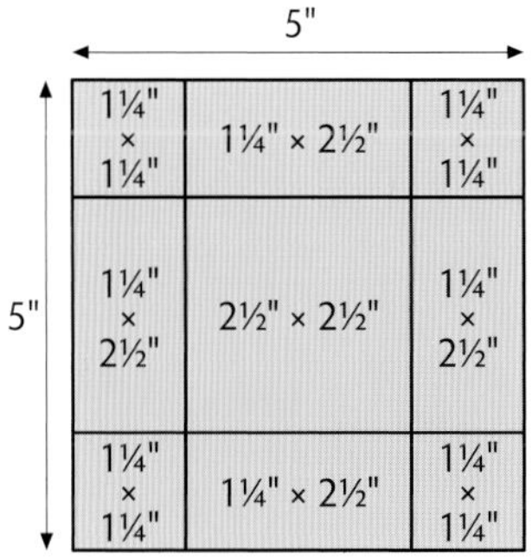

	5"	
1¼" × 1¼"	1¼" × 2½"	1¼" × 1¼"
1¼" × 2½"	2½" × 2½"	1¼" × 2½"
1¼" × 1¼"	1¼" × 2½"	1¼" × 1¼"

Cutting diagram

Continued on page 34

Continued from page 33

From white print A, cut:

9 strips, 1¼" × 42"; crosscut into 128 rectangles, 1¼" × 2½"

From white print B, cut:

2 strips, 2½" × 42"; crosscut into 31 squares, 2½" × 2½"

4 strips, 1¼" × 42"; crosscut into 124 squares, 1¼" × 1¼"

From the green floral, cut:

4 strips, 3" × 42"; crosscut into:
  2 strips, 3" × 32"
  2 strips, 3" × 30"

From the pink gingham, cut:

4 strips, 2" × 42"

MAKING THE BLOCKS

Press all seam allowances as indicated by the arrows.

1. Lay out four white 1¼" × 2½" rectangles, four matching print 1¼" squares, and one print 2½" square in three rows as shown; the 2½" square should match the small squares. Sew together the pieces in each row, then join the rows to make block A, which measures 4" square, including seam allowances. Repeat to make 32 of block A.

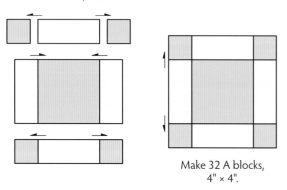

Make 32 A blocks, 4" × 4".

2. Lay out four matching print 1¼" × 2½" rectangles, four white 1¼" squares, and one white 2½" square in three rows as shown. Sew together the pieces in each row, then join the rows to make block B, which measures 4" square, including seam allowances. Repeat to make 31 of block B.

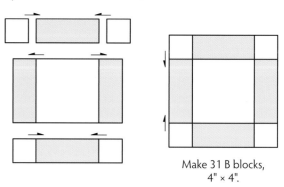

Make 31 B blocks, 4" × 4".

ASSEMBLING THE QUILT TOP

Alternating blocks A and B, lay out the blocks in nine rows of seven blocks each. Join the blocks in each row, then join the rows to make the quilt center measuring 25" × 32", including seam allowances.

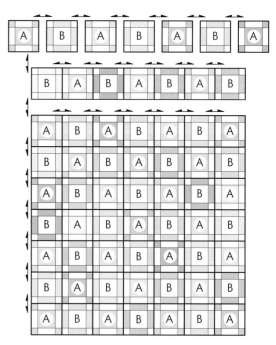

Quilt assembly

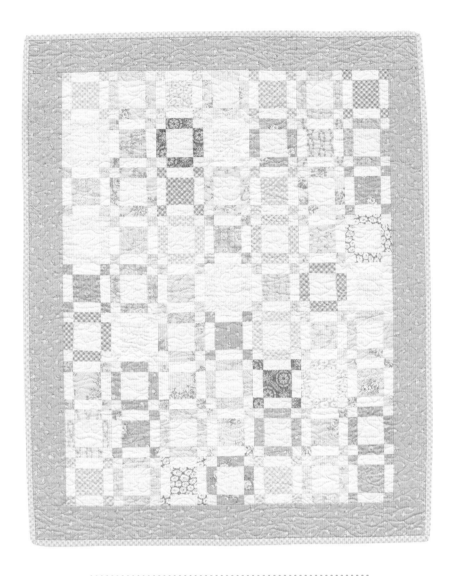

Designed, pieced, and quilted by Brenda Riddle

ADDING THE BORDER

Sew the green floral 3" × 32" strips to the sides of the quilt top. Sew the green floral 3" × 30" strips to the top and bottom edges to complete the quilt top. Press the seam allowances toward the border.

FINISHING THE QUILT

For more details on any finishing steps, visit ShopMartingale.com/HowtoQuilt for free, downloadable information.

1. Layer the backing, batting, and quilt top; baste the layers together.

2. Quilt by hand or machine. The quilt shown is machine quilted with an allover wavy design.

3. Use the pink gingham 2"-wide strips to make binding, and then attach the binding to the quilt.

Puddin' Pie

*I*nspiration can come from anywhere. A few years ago, I was in Norway doing some trunk shows and workshops, and this was the design on the floor tiles in a tiny little bakery. I loved it then and still do now!

QUILT SIZE: 58½" × 58½"
BLOCK SIZE: 12" × 12"

MATERIALS

Yardage is based on 42"-wide fabric. Fat quarters measure 18" × 21".

- 6 fat quarters of assorted blue prints for blocks
- 2¼ yards of cream solid for blocks and sashing
- ⅔ yard of green print for blocks and sashing
- 1⅛ yards of light green gingham for blocks and sashing
- ⅛ yard *each* of 5 assorted pink prints for blocks and sashing
- ⅛ yard *each* of 3 assorted light prints for blocks
- 1 yard of light floral for sashing
- Scraps of assorted yellow prints for sashing
- ⅝ yard of blue gingham for binding
- 3⅔ yards of fabric for backing
- 65" × 65" square of batting

CUTTING

All measurements include ¼" seam allowances.

From *each* of the 6 assorted blue prints, cut:
3 strips, 4½" × 21"; crosscut into 12 squares, 4½" × 4½" (72 total; 8 are extra)

From the cream solid, cut:
2 strips, 3½" × 42"; crosscut into 20 squares, 3½" × 3½"
26 strips, 2½" × 42"; crosscut into 384 squares, 2½" × 2½"

From the green print, cut:
4 strips, 4½" × 42"; crosscut into 28 squares, 4½" × 4½"
1 strip, 2½" × 42"; crosscut into 8 squares, 2½" × 2½"

From the light green gingham, cut:
5 strips, 4½" × 42"; crosscut into 36 squares, 4½" × 4½"
4 strips, 3½" × 42"; crosscut into 40 squares, 3½" × 3½"

From *each* of the 5 assorted pink prints, cut:
1 strip, 3" × 42"; crosscut into:
  8 squares, 3" × 3" (40 total); cut each square in half diagonally to make 16 triangles (80 total; 16 are extra)
  4 squares, 2½" × 2½" (20 total)

Continued on page 39

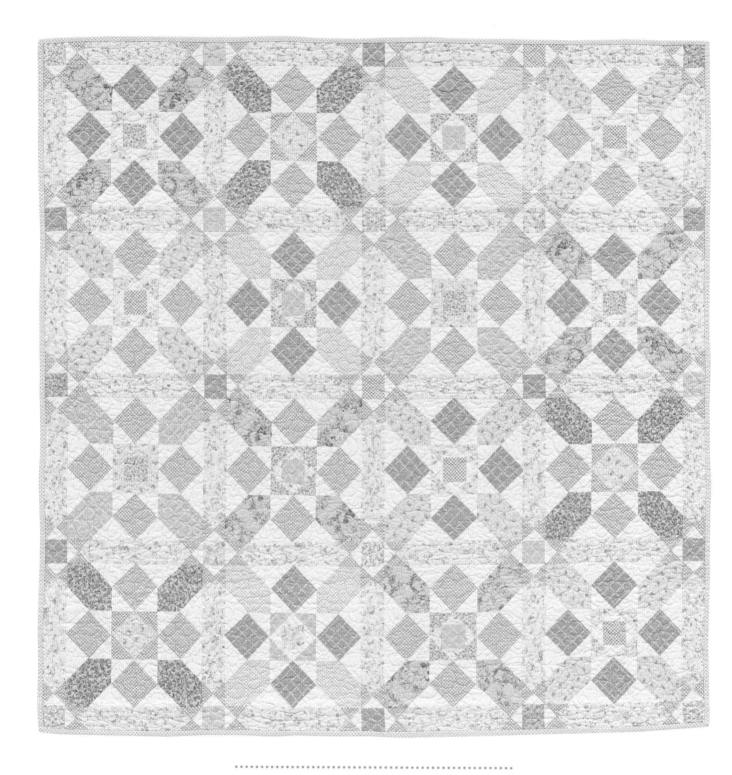

Designed and pieced by Brenda Riddle; quilted by Bob Jensen

Continued from page 37

From *each* of the 3 assorted light prints, cut:

1 strip, 2½" × 42"; cut into:
   3 squares, 2½" × 2½" (9 total; 2 are extra)
   12 squares, 2⅜" × 2⅜" (36 total); cut each
      square in half diagonally to make 24 triangles
      (72 total; 8 are extra)

From the light floral, cut:

3 strips, 8½" × 42"; crosscut into 40 rectangles,
   2½" × 8½"
2 strips, 3½" × 42"; crosscut into 20 squares,
   3½" × 3½"

From the assorted yellow prints, cut:

6 squares, 2½" × 2½"

From the blue gingham, cut:

7 strips, 2½" × 42"

MAKING THE BLOCKS

Press all seam allowances as indicated by the arrows.

1. Place a cream 2½" square right sides together on one corner of a blue 4½" square and sew diagonally as shown. Trim off the outer triangle corner, leaving a ¼" seam allowance, and press open. Repeat to add a second cream 2½" square to the opposite corner in the same manner. Trim and press as before to make unit A, which should be 4½" square, including seam allowances. Make 64 of unit A (16 sets of 4 matching units).

Make 64 A units
(16 sets of 4),
4½" × 4½".

2. Place a cream 2½" square right sides together on one corner of a green 4½" square and sew diagonally as shown. Trim off the outer triangle corner, leaving a ¼" seam allowance, and press open. Repeat to add cream 2½" squares to the remaining three corners in the same manner. Trim and press as before to make unit B, which should be 4½" square, including seam allowances. Make 64 of unit B (16 sets of 4 matching units) using both the green print and light green gingham 4½" squares.

Make 64 B units
(16 sets of 4),
4½" × 4½".

3. Center and sew the long edges of two matching light triangles to opposite edges of a pink 2½" square. (Take care when handling the triangles so as not to stretch the cut bias edge.) Add two more matching light triangles to the remaining edges.

4. Center and sew two matching pink triangles to opposite edges of the step 3 square. Add two more matching pink triangles to the remaining edges to make unit C, which should measure 4½" square, including seam allowances. Make 16 of unit C.

Make 16 C units,
4½" × 4½".

5. Lay out four matching A units, four matching B units, and one C unit in three rows as shown. Sew the units into rows, and then join the rows to make a block, which should measure 12½" square, including seam allowances. Make 16 blocks.

Make 16 blocks,
12½" × 12½".

MAKING THE SASHING

1. Mark a diagonal line on the wrong side of each green gingham 3½" square.

2. With right sides together, place a marked square on a cream 3½" square and sew ¼" from each side of the drawn line. Cut along the drawn line and press open to make two half-square-triangle units. Repeat to make 40 matching units.

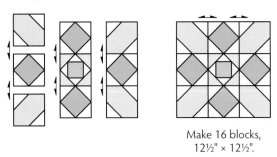

Make 40 units,
3⅛" × 3⅛".

3. Using light floral 3½" squares instead of cream squares, repeat step 2 to make 40 additional half-square-triangle units. On the wrong side of each of these units, mark a diagonal line from corner to corner.

4. With right sides together, place a marked half-square-triangle unit on an unmarked unit from step 2 (the green gingham triangles should not face each other; they should face the cream and light floral triangles). Sew ¼" from each side of the drawn line. Cut along the drawn line and press the seam allowances open. Center and trim each quarter-square-triangle unit to measure 2½" square, including seam allowances. Make 80 units total.

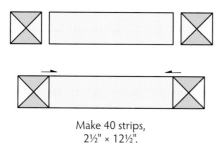

Make 80 units.

5. Matching the light floral edges, sew a quarter-square-triangle unit to each end of a light floral 2½" × 8½" rectangle to make a sashing strip. Make 40 sashing strips total.

Make 40 strips,
2½" × 12½".

ASSEMBLING THE QUILT TOP

Lay out the remaining assorted 2½" squares, sashing strips, and blocks in nine rows as shown below. Sew together the pieces in each row. Join the rows to make the quilt top.

FINISHING THE QUILT

For more details on any finishing steps, visit ShopMartingale.com/HowtoQuilt for free, downloadable information.

1. Layer the backing, batting, and quilt top; baste the layers together.

2. Quilt by hand or machine. The quilt shown is machine quilted with an allover feather design.

3. Use the blue gingham 2½"-wide strips to make binding, and then attach the binding to the quilt.

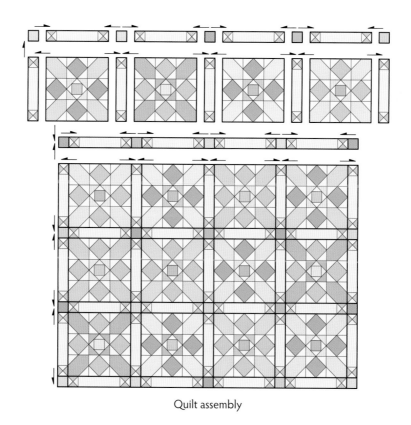

Quilt assembly

Snowflake Fleurs

Snowflake Fleurs and Mini Fleurs on page 51 were inspired by one of the beautiful vintage quilts from the "Infinite Variety: Red and White Quilts" exhibition. The original quilt was white appliqué on a red background; I chose to use a light background for my quilts, with either multicolored or red-and-green appliqué.

QUILT SIZE: 50" × 50"
BLOCK SIZE: 9" × 9"

MATERIALS

Yardage is based on 42"-wide fabric. Fat eighths measure 9" × 21".

- ⅛ yard or fat eighth *each* of 16 assorted prints for appliqués
- ⅛ yard or fat eighth *each* of 2 different green prints for border appliqués
- 2⅜ yards of white tone on tone for block backgrounds and border
- ½ yard of light floral for binding
- 3¼ yards of fabric for backing*
- 56" × 56" square of batting
- 3 yards of lightweight fusible web, such as Steam-a-Seam Lite

*Or 1⅔ yards of 80"-wide fabric.

CUTTING

All measurements include ¼" seam allowances.

From the white tone on tone, cut:
4 strips, 10" × 42"; crosscut into 16 squares, 10" × 10"
5 strips, 7¼" × 42"; crosscut *2 of the strips* into 2 strips, 7¼" × 36½"

From the light floral, cut:
6 strips, 2½" × 42"

Designed and appliquéd by Brenda Riddle; quilted by Karolyn "Nubin" Jensen

APPLIQUÉING THE BLOCKS

1. Use the patterns on page 48 to trace the leaves, plumes, petals, and flower centers onto fusible web the number of times indicated on each pattern. Leave ½" between tracings.

2. Following the instructions for "Fusible Appliqué" on page 94, press a set of fusible-web shapes for one block onto the wrong side of each assorted print: four plumes, eight petals, four leaves, four reversed leaves, and one flower center. Cut out each fabric shape on the drawn line. Peel off the paper backing.

3. On each white 10" background square, lightly mark ¼" from each side for the final cutting size for the appliqué blocks. (The background squares will be trimmed to 9½" square after appliqué is completed.)

4. Referring to the block appliqué layout on page 49, position a set of matching print appliqués on a marked white 10" square, being sure all of the appliqués are at least ¼" within the marked lines. Fuse in place following the manufacturer's instructions. Using thread to match the appliqués and a small blanket stitch, machine sew around each appliqué shape. Trim the block on the drawn lines so it measures 9½" square, including seam allowances. Repeat to make 16 appliquéd blocks.

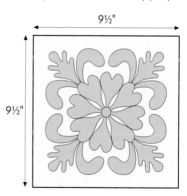

Make 16 blocks.

ASSEMBLING THE QUILT TOP

Press all seam allowances as indicated by the arrows. Join the blocks in four rows of four blocks each. Join the rows to make the quilt center, which should measure 36½" square, including seam allowances.

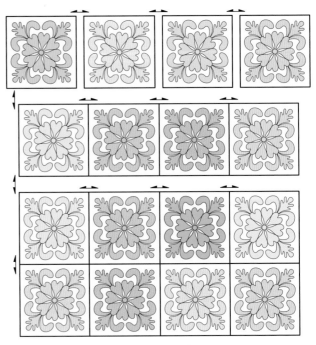

Quilt assembly

APPLIQUÉING AND ADDING THE BORDER

1. Use the patterns on page 48 to trace the border leaves and border plumes onto fusible web the number of times indicated on each pattern. Leave ½" between tracings.

2. Following the instructions for "Fusible Appliqué," press the plumes onto one green print and the leaves onto the second green print. Cut out each fabric shape on the drawn line. Peel off the paper backing.

3. On each white 7¼" × 36½" strip, lightly mark ¼" from each end to assist in the placement of the corner leaves. Referring to the diagram on page 47, position four leaves, four reversed leaves, and three plumes on each strip. (Make sure the tips of the

leaves and plumes are placed at the edge of the strip so they'll be included in the border seamlines.) Then fuse in place following the manufacturer's instructions. Using thread to match the appliqués and a small blanket stitch, machine sew around each appliqué. Make two appliquéd side borders.

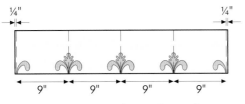

Make 2 side borders, 7¼" × 36½".

4. Trim the selvages off the three white 7¼" × 42" strips and sew them together end to end. From this long strip, cut two lengths, 50".

5. On each white 7¼" × 50" strip, lightly draw a line 7" from each end to assist in the placement of the corner leaves and plumes. Referring to the diagram below, position four leaves, four reversed leaves, and five plumes on each strip. (Make sure that the tips of the leaves and plumes are placed at the edge of the strip so they'll be included in the border seamlines.) Then fuse in place following the manufacturer's instructions. Using thread to match the appliqués and a small blanket stitch, machine sew around each appliqué. Make two appliquéd top/bottom borders.

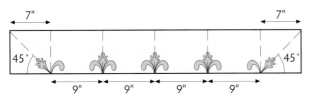

Make 2 top/bottom borders, 7¼" × 50".

6. Sew the side borders to each side of the quilt center. Sew the top/bottom borders to the top and bottom edges of the quilt center to complete the quilt top.

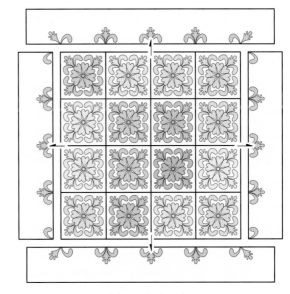

Adding the border

FINISHING THE QUILT

For more details on any finishing steps, visit ShopMartingale.com/HowtoQuilt for free, downloadable information.

1. Layer the backing, batting, and quilt top; baste the layers together.

2. Quilt by hand or machine. The quilt shown is machine quilted with outline quilting around all the appliqué elements and tiny overall feathers in the background.

3. Use the light floral 2½"-wide strips to make binding, and then attach the binding to the quilt.

Plume

Large quilt: Cut 4 from each assorted print (64 total).
Mini-quilt: Cut 4 from each red print, green print, and green gingham (16 total).

Petal

Large quilt: Cut 8 from each assorted print (128 total).
Mini-quilt: Cut 8 from each red print, green print, and green gingham (32 total).

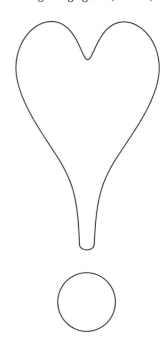

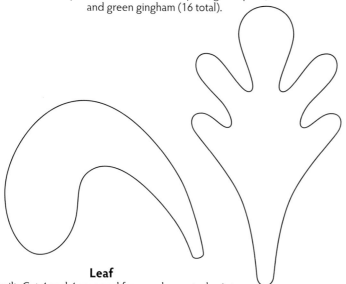

Leaf

Large quilt: Cut 4 and 4 reversed from each assorted print (64 total of leaf and leaf reversed).
Mini-quilt: Cut 4 and 4 reversed from each red print, green print, and green gingham (16 total of leaf and leaf reversed).

Flower center

Large quilt: Cut 1 from each assorted print (16 total).
Mini-quilt: Cut 1 from each red print, green print, and green gingham (4 total).

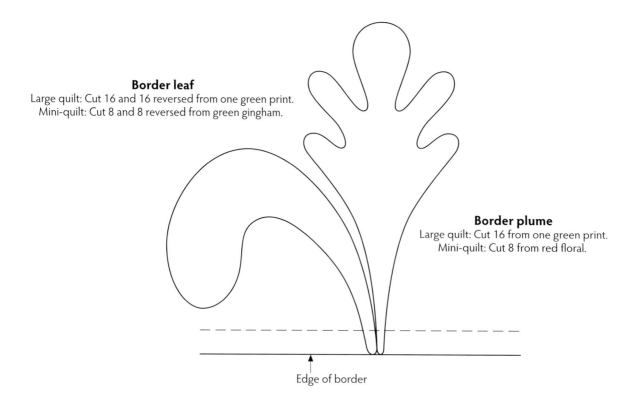

Border leaf

Large quilt: Cut 16 and 16 reversed from one green print.
Mini-quilt: Cut 8 and 8 reversed from green gingham.

Border plume

Large quilt: Cut 16 from one green print.
Mini-quilt: Cut 8 from red floral.

Edge of border

Block appliqué layout

Designed, appliquéd, and quilted by Brenda Riddle

Mini Fleurs

*F*ollow these directions for the red-and-green mini-quilt. My favorite thing about this quilt is that the red and green prints make it perfect for Christmas, but because the fabrics are simple florals and gingham, I can use this quilt for decorating year-round.

QUILT SIZE: 28" × 28"
BLOCK SIZE: 9" × 9"

MATERIALS

Yardage is based on 42"-wide fabric. Fat eighths measure 9" × 21".

- ⅛ yard or fat eighth *each* of 2 different red prints for block appliqués
- ⅛ yard or fat eighth of green print for block appliqués
- ¼ yard of green gingham for block and border appliqués
- ⅜ yard of red floral for border appliqués and binding
- ¾ yard of white tone on tone for block backgrounds and border
- 1 yard of fabric for backing
- 32" × 32" square of batting
- 1½ yards of lightweight fusible web, such as Steam-a-Seam Lite

CUTTING

All measurements include ¼" seam allowances.

From the white tone on tone, cut:
1 strip, 10" × 42"; crosscut into 4 squares, 10" × 10"
3 strips, 5¼" × 42"; crosscut into:
    2 strips, 5¼" × 28"
    2 strips, 5¼" × 18½"

From the red floral, cut:
3 strips, 2" × 42"

APPLIQUÉING THE BLOCKS

1. Use the patterns on page 48 to trace the leaves, plumes, petals, and flower centers onto fusible web the number of times indicated on each pattern. Leave ½" between tracings.

2. Following the instructions for "Fusible Appliqué" on page 94, press a set of fusible-web shapes for one block onto the wrong side of each red print, the green print, and the green gingham: four plumes, eight petals, four leaves, four reversed leaves, and one flower center. Cut out each fabric shape on the drawn line. Peel off the paper backing.

3. On each white 10" background square, lightly mark ¼" from each side for the final cutting size for the appliqué blocks. (The background squares will be trimmed to 9½" square after appliqué is completed.)

4. Referring to the block appliqué layout on page 49, position a set of matching print appliqués on a marked white 10" square, being sure all of the appliqués are at least ¼" within the marked lines. Fuse in place following the manufacturer's instructions. Using thread to match the appliqués and a small blanket stitch, machine sew around each appliqué shape. Trim the block on the drawn lines so it measures 9½" square, including seam allowances. Repeat to make four appliquéd blocks.

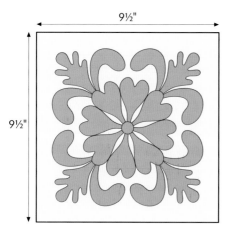

Make 4 blocks.

ASSEMBLING THE QUILT TOP

Press all seam allowances as indicated by the arrows. Join the blocks in two rows of two blocks each. Join the rows to make the quilt center, which should measure 18½" square, including seam allowances.

Quilt assembly

APPLIQUÉING AND ADDING THE BORDER

1. Use the patterns on page 48 to trace the border leaves and border plumes onto fusible web, according to the totals on the patterns. Leave ½" between tracings.

2. Following the instructions for "Fusible Appliqué," press the plumes onto the red floral and the leaves onto the green gingham. Cut out each fabric shape on the drawn line. Peel off the paper backing.

3. On each white 5¼" × 18½" strip, lightly mark ¼" from each end to assist in the placement of the corner leaves. Referring to the diagram on page 53, position two leaves, two reversed leaves, and one plume on each strip. (Make sure the tips of the leaves and plumes are placed at the edge of the strip so they'll be included in the border seamlines.) Then fuse in place following the manufacturer's

instructions. Using thread to match the appliqués and a small blanket stitch, machine sew around each appliqué. Make two appliquéd side borders.

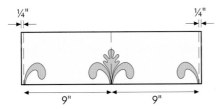

Make 2 side borders, 5¼" × 18½".

4. On each white 5¼" × 28" strip, lightly draw a line 5" from each end to assist in the placement of the corner leaves and plumes. Referring to the diagram below, position two leaves, two reversed leaves, and three plumes on each strip. (Make sure the tips of the leaves and plumes are placed at the edge of the strip so they'll be included in the border seamlines.) Then fuse in place following the manufacturer's instructions. Using thread to match the appliqués and a small blanket stitch, machine sew around each appliqué. Make two appliquéd top/bottom borders.

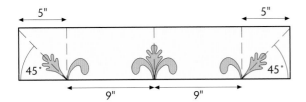

Make 2 top/bottom borders, 5¼" × 28".

5. Sew the side borders to each side of the quilt center. Sew the top/bottom borders to the top and bottom edges of the quilt center to complete the quilt top.

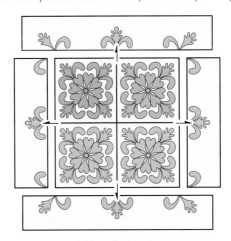

Adding the border

FINISHING THE QUILT

For more details on any finishing steps, visit ShopMartingale.com/HowtoQuilt for free, downloadable information.

1. Layer the backing, batting, and quilt top; baste the layers together.

2. Quilt by hand or machine. The quilt shown is machine quilted with outline quilting around all the appliqué elements and a small stipple in the background.

3. Use the red floral 2"-wide strips to make binding, and then attach the binding to the quilt.

Blissful

I love that Blissful's design is based on a vintage block, and I also love that the blocks are the perfect size to use up small bits of fabrics you've saved or to feature a favorite collection of fabrics you treasure.

QUILT SIZE: 26" × 26"
BLOCK SIZE: 6" × 6"

MATERIALS

Yardage is based on 42"-wide fabric.

- 1 yard of off-white tone on tone for block backgrounds and setting squares and triangles
- 9 squares, 10" × 10", of assorted green, blue, pink, and yellow prints for blocks
- ¼ yard of blue gingham for binding
- ⅞ yard of fabric for backing
- 30" × 30" square of batting

CUTTING

All measurements include ¼" seam allowances.

From the off-white tone on tone, cut:
1 strip, 9¾" × 42"; crosscut into:
 2 squares, 9¾" × 9¾"; cut the squares
  into quarters diagonally to make 8
  setting triangles
 2 squares, 5¼" × 5¼"; cut the squares in half
  diagonally to make 4 corner triangles
1 strip, 6½" × 42"; crosscut into 4 squares,
 6½" × 6½"
2 strips, 2" × 42"; crosscut into 36 squares, 2" × 2"
7 strips, 1½" × 42"; crosscut into:
 72 rectangles, 1½" × 2½"
 36 squares, 1½" × 1½"

From *each* 10" square, cut:
1 square, 2½" × 2½" (9 total)
4 squares, 2" × 2" (36 total)
12 squares, 1½" × 1½" (108 total)

From the blue gingham, cut:
3 strips, 2" × 42"

Designed and pieced by Brenda Riddle; quilted by Karolyn "Nubin" Jensen

MAKING THE BLOCKS

Press all seam allowances as indicated by the arrows.

1. Draw a diagonal line on the wrong side of each off-white 2" square.

2. Place a marked 2" square on top of a print 2" square with right sides together and sew ¼" from each side of the drawn line. Cut along the drawn line to make two triangles. Press open to make two half-square-triangle units. Trim each to 1½" square, including seam allowances. Repeat to make 72 half-square-triangle units (nine sets of eight matching units).

Make 72 units.

3. Matching the prints, sew one print 1½" square, one off-white 1½" square, and two half-square-triangle units as shown to make a corner unit. The unit should measure 2½" square, including seam allowances. Repeat to make 36 corner units (nine sets of four matching units).

Make 9 sets of
4 matching corner units,
2½" × 2½".

4. Place a print 1½" square right side down on one end of an off-white 1½" × 2½" rectangle. Sew diagonally through the center as shown. Trim off the outer corner, leaving a ¼" seam allowance. Press the remaining triangle back. Using a matching print 1½" square, repeat this step on the other end of the rectangle to make a flying-geese unit. Repeat to make 36 flying-geese units (nine sets of four matching units).

Make 9 sets of 4
matching flying-geese units,
1½" × 2½".

5. Sew an off-white 1½" × 2½" rectangle to the top of each flying-geese unit as shown to make a side unit, which should measure 2½" square, including seam allowances. Repeat to make 36 side units total (nine sets of four matching units).

Make 9 sets of
4 matching side units,
2½" × 2½".

6. Matching the prints, lay out four corner units, four side units, and one print 2½" square in three rows. Sew together the pieces in each row, then join the rows to make a block that measures 6½" square, including seam allowances. Repeat to make nine blocks.

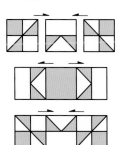 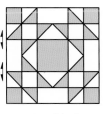

Make 9 blocks,
6½" × 6½".

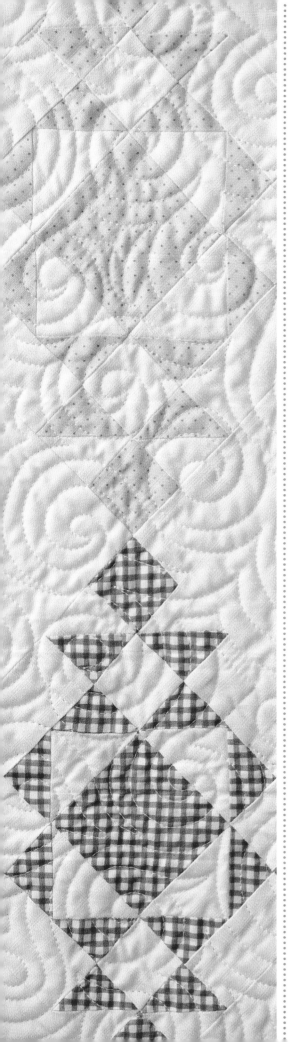

ASSEMBLING THE QUILT TOP

Referring to the quilt assembly diagram below, lay out the blocks and off-white setting squares and triangles as shown. Join the pieces in each row, lining up the bottoms of the blocks and setting triangles. Sew the rows together, lining up the block seams. Sew an off-white corner triangle to each corner of the quilt center to complete the quilt top.

Quilt assembly

FINISHING THE QUILT

For more details on any finishing steps, you can visit ShopMartingale.com/HowtoQuilt for free, downloadable information.

1. Layer the backing, batting, and quilt top; baste the layers together.

2. Quilt by hand or machine. The quilt shown is machine quilted with an allover swirl pattern.

3. Use the blue gingham 2"-wide strips to make binding, and then attach the binding to the quilt.

Nesting

*L*ittle bluebirds happily gather pretties for sprucing up their nests. The appliqué is surrounded by squares in a gingham pattern and a sweet, easy-to-stitch scallop border, resulting in a quilt that's guaranteed to make you smile. Bring it out when you're in a nesting mood.

QUILT SIZE: 44½" × 44½"

MATERIALS

Yardage is based on 42"-wide fabric.

- ⅓ yard of cream tone on tone for bluebird background
- ⅜ yard *each* of cream floral A and pink floral for patchwork
- ¾ yard of cream floral B for middle border and scallop
- ⅜ yard *each* of green tone on tone and green floral for patchwork
- ¼ yard of blue floral A for flange, inner border, and bluebird back wings
- ⅝ yard of blue floral B for outer border and bluebirds
- Scrap of light brown print for bluebird breasts
- ½ yard of blue diagonal stripe for binding
- 2⅞ yards of fabric for backing
- 51" × 51" square of batting
- ⅔ yard of lightweight fusible web, such as Steam-a-Seam Lite
- Embroidery floss: rose, dark rose, yellow, aqua, green, and gold
- Brown .01 Pigma pen or fine mechanical pencil

CUTTING

All measurements include ¼" seam allowances.

From the cream tone on tone, cut:
1 rectangle, 9" × 18"

From cream floral A, cut:
4 strips, 2½" × 42"; crosscut *1 of the strips* into:
  2 strips, 2½" × 11"
  4 squares, 2½" × 2½"

From the pink floral, cut:
4 strips, 2½" × 42"; crosscut *1 of the strips* into:
  1 strip, 2½" × 11"
  4 squares, 2½" × 2½"

From cream floral B, cut:
4 strips, 3" × 42"; crosscut into:
  2 strips, 3" × 36½"
  2 strips, 3" × 31½"
4 strips, 2½" × 42"

From the green tone on tone, cut:
4 strips, 2½" × 42"; crosscut *1 of the strips* into:
  1 strip, 2½" × 11"
  4 squares, 2½" × 2½"

From the green floral, cut:
4 strips, 2½" × 42"; crosscut *1 of the strips* into:
  2 strips, 2½" × 11"
  4 squares, 2½" × 2½"

From blue floral A, cut:
6 strips, 1" × 42"; crosscut *4 of the strips* into:
  2 strips, 1" × 31½"
  2 strips, 1" × 30½"

From blue floral B, cut:
4 strips, 4½" × 42"; crosscut into 4 strips,
    4½" × 36½"

From the blue diagonal stripe, cut:
5 strips, 2½" × 42"

EMBROIDERING AND APPLIQUÉING THE CENTER RECTANGLE

1. The bluebirds embroidery pattern is on page 66. Using a brown .01 Pigma pen or fine mechanical pencil, center and trace the flowers and vines of the embroidery pattern onto the cream 9" × 18" rectangle using a light box or sunlit window. (The bluebird appliqués will be added later.)

2. For vines and straight lines, use either a stem stitch or a backstitch. (The stem stitch has a thicker appearance; backstitch is more delicate.) Flowers and leaves are made with lazy daisy stitches, and the flower centers are filled in with French knots. See the photo on page 63 for floss colors, the embroidery pattern for stitch placement, and "Embroidery Stitches" on page 95 for instructions.

3. Use the patterns on page 67 to trace three bluebirds, six wings, and three breasts onto fusible web, leaving ½" between tracings.

4. Following the instructions for "Fusible Appliqué" on page 94, press each fusible-web shape onto the wrong side of blue floral A, blue floral B, or brown print. Cut out each fabric shape on the drawn line. Peel off the paper backing.

5. Place the appliqués on the cream 9" × 18" rectangle and fuse following the manufacturer's instructions. Using thread to match the appliqués and a small blanket stitch, machine sew around each appliqué.

6. After the bluebird appliqué is complete, satin stitch the beaks and eyes.

7. When embroidery and appliqué are complete, press the center rectangle; trim it to 6½" × 14½".

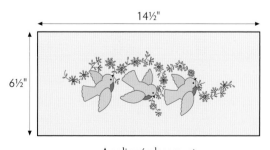

Appliqué placement

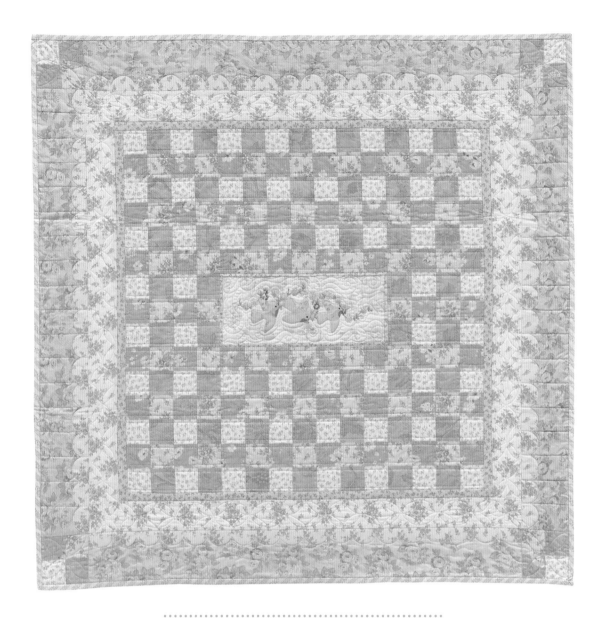

Designed and pieced by Brenda Riddle; quilted by Karolyn "Nubin" Jensen

8. With wrong sides together, fold two blue floral A 1" × 42" strips in half lengthwise to measure ½" wide. (If your fabric is wider than 42", you may need only one strip.) From these folded strips, cut two 6½"-long pieces and two 14½"-long pieces.

9. Position a 6½"-long piece on each end of the embroidered rectangle, lining up the raw edges and making sure the folded edge is toward the center. Baste the blue strips in place, ¼" from the edges. Repeat with the 14½" pieces, basting them to the top and bottom of the embroidered rectangle.

Folded edges.

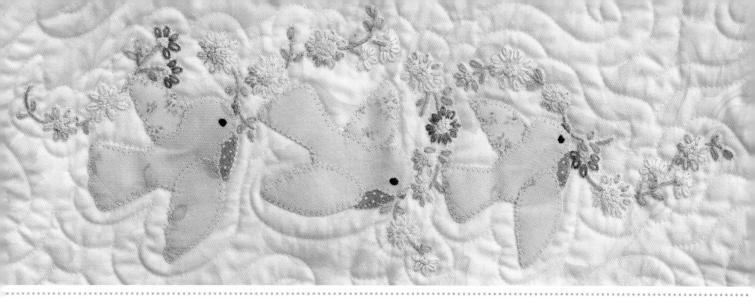

ASSEMBLING THE QUILT CENTER

Press all seam allowances as indicated by the arrows.

1. Sew together three cream floral A and three green tone-on-tone 2½" × 42" strips as shown to make strip set A. From this strip set, cut 16 A segments, 2½" wide.

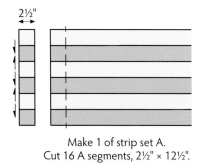

Make 1 of strip set A.
Cut 16 A segments, 2½" × 12½".

2. Join three green floral and three pink floral 2½" × 42" strips as shown to make strip set B. Cut 14 B segments, 2½" wide.

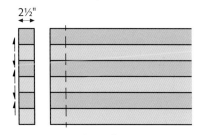

Make 1 of strip set B.
Cut 14 B segments, 2½" × 12½".

3. Join eight A segments and seven B segments to make a gingham large rectangle, which should be 12½" × 30½", including seam allowances. Make two.

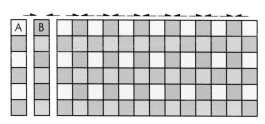

Make 2 gingham large rectangles,
12½" × 30½".

4. Sew together one green tone-on-tone and two cream floral A 2½" × 11" strips to make strip set C. From this strip set, cut four C segments, 2½" wide.

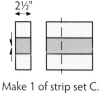

Make 1 of strip set C.
Cut 4 C segments, 2½" × 6½".

5. Sew together one pink floral and two green floral 2½" × 11" strips to make strip set D. From this strip set, cut four D segments, 2½" wide.

Make 1 of strip set D.
Cut 4 D segments, 2½" × 6½".

6. Join two C segments and two D segments to make a gingham small rectangle, which should be 6½" × 8½", including seam allowances. Make two.

Make 2 gingham small rectangles, 6½" × 8½".

7. Sew the small gingham rectangles to the sides of the embroidered rectangle, making sure the green-and-pink edges are next to the embroidery center. Sew the large gingham rectangles to the top and bottom of the embroidery center, making sure the green-and-pink edges are next to the embroidery center. The quilt center should measure 30½" square, including seam allowances.

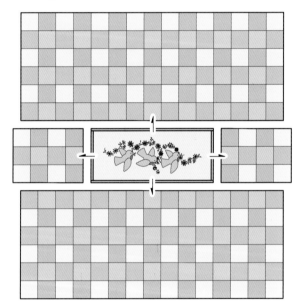

Quilt assembly

ADDING THE BORDERS

1. Sew the blue floral A 1" × 30½" strips to the sides of the quilt center. Sew the blue floral A 1" × 31½" strips to the top and bottom edges of the quilt center.

2. Sew the cream floral B 3" × 31½" strips to the sides of the quilt center. Sew the cream floral B 3" × 36½" strips to the top and bottom edges of the quilt center.

3. Use the scallop pattern on page 67 to trace four border sections of 18 scallops each onto fusible web, leaving ½" between tracings. These do not have to be a single long strip of 18 scallops each, but can be pieced from several pieces of fusible web to equal 18 scallops.

4. Following the instructions for "Fusible Appliqué," press each fusible-web 18-scallop section onto the wrong side of a cream floral B 2½" × 42" strip. Cut out the scallops on the drawn line. Peel off the paper backing.

5. Position a scallop strip along one edge of a blue floral B 4½" × 36½" strip, ¼" from each end. Fuse in place following the manufacturer's instructions. Using thread to match the appliqués and a small blanket stitch, machine sew around the curved edge of each appliqué. Repeat to make four blue border sections.

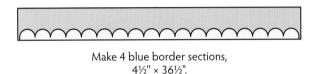

Make 4 blue border sections,
4½" × 36½".

6. Sew together one cream floral A 2½" square, one green tone-on-tone 2½" square, one green floral 2½" square, and one pink floral 2½" square in pairs as shown. Join the pairs to make a four-patch unit, which should measure 4½" square, including seam allowances. Repeat to make four matching four-patch units.

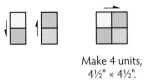

Make 4 units,
4½" × 4½".

7. Sew blue border sections to opposite edges of the quilt center. Sew a four-patch unit to each end of the remaining blue border sections. Sew these strips to the top and bottom edges of the quilt center to complete the quilt top.

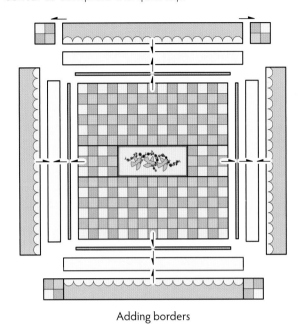

Adding borders

FINISHING THE QUILT

For more details on any finishing steps, visit ShopMartingale.com/HowtoQuilt for free, downloadable information.

1. Layer the backing, batting, and quilt top; baste the layers together.

2. Quilt by hand or machine. The quilt shown is machine quilted with wavy lines in the background of the embroidery, horizontal lines through the gingham piecing and outer border, and a pumpkin-seed design in the cream middle border and four-patch units.

3. Use the blue stripe 2½"-wide strips to make binding, and then attach the binding to the quilt.

Connect along dashed line to complete pattern.

Connect along dashed line to complete pattern.

Embroidery key

● French knot

◠ Lazy daisy

■ Satin stitch

— Stem stitch

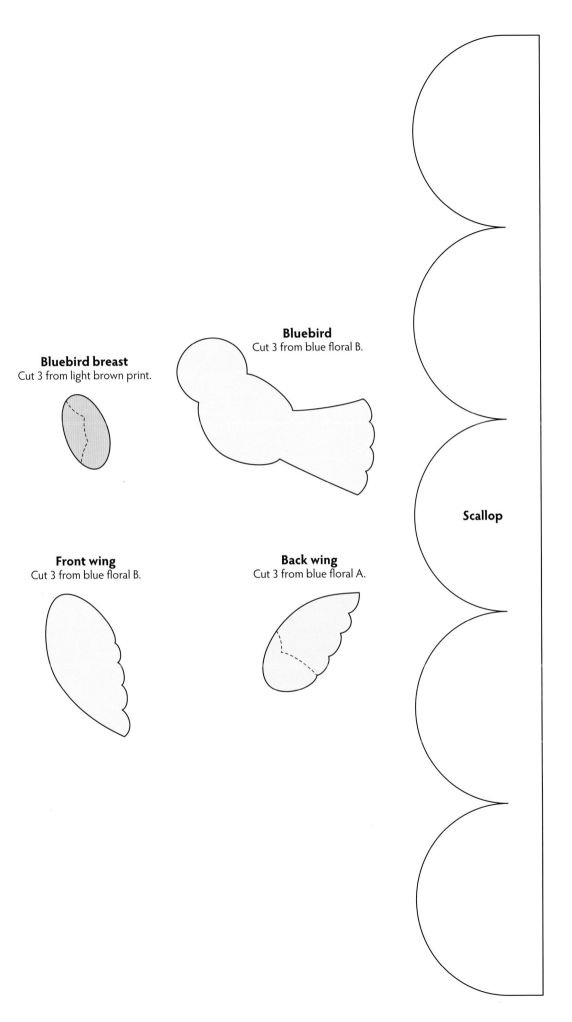

Bluebird breast
Cut 3 from light brown print.

Bluebird
Cut 3 from blue floral B.

Scallop

Front wing
Cut 3 from blue floral B.

Back wing
Cut 3 from blue floral A.

Coventry

A classic Star block always lends an air of both comfort and sophistication. Here, Ohio Star blocks are placed with white setting squares, giving the quilt an airy look, and the dotted borders add a dash of fun.

QUILT SIZE: 61¼" × 73¼"
BLOCK SIZE: 6" × 6"

MATERIALS

Yardage is based on 42"-wide fabric. Fat quarters measure 18" × 21".

- 13 fat quarters of assorted blue, yellow, pink, tan, and green prints for blocks
- 4⅝ yards of white tone on tone for blocks, setting squares, and borders
- ⅜ yard of light blue gingham for borders
- ⅝ yard of light blue print for binding
- 4½ yards of fabric for backing
- 68" × 80" piece of batting

CUTTING

All measurements include ¼" seam allowances.

From *each* assorted print fat quarter, cut:
1 strip, 3½" × 21"; crosscut into 3 squares,
    3½" × 3½" (39 total; 3 are extra)
3 strips, 2" × 21"; crosscut into 24 squares, 2" × 2"
    (312 total; 24 are extra)

From the white tone on tone, cut:
6 strips, 6½" × 42"; crosscut into 31 squares,
    6½" × 6½"
6 strips, 4" × 42"
6 strips, 3" × 42"
5 strips, 2⅜" × 42"
21 strips, 2" × 42"; crosscut into:
    144 rectangles, 2" × 3½"
    144 squares, 2" × 2"
11 strips, 1¼" × 42"; crosscut *2 of the strips* into:
    4 strips, 1¼" × 7¼"
    4 strips, 1¼" × 6½"

Continued on page 71

Designed and pieced by Brenda Riddle; quilted by Nicole Christoffersen

Continued from page 69

From the light blue gingham, cut:

9 strips, 1¼" × 42"

From the light blue print, cut:

8 strips, 2½" × 42"

MAKING THE BLOCKS

Press all seam allowances as indicated by the arrows.

1. Draw a diagonal line on the wrong side of eight matching print 2" squares.

2. Place a marked 2" square, right sides together, on one end of a white 2" × 3½" rectangle as shown. Sew on the drawn line. Trim off the outer corner, leaving a ¼" seam allowance, and press open. Add a second marked 2" square to the remaining end of the rectangle as before to make a star-point unit. Repeat to make four matching star-point units.

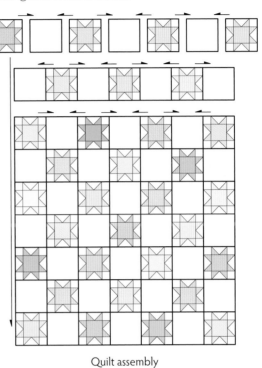

Make 4 units,
2" × 3½".

3. Lay out four white 2" squares, four matching star-point units, and one print 3½" square in three rows as shown; the 3½" square should match the print in the star-point units. Join the pieces in each row, then join the rows to make an Ohio Star block. The block should measure 6½" square, including seam allowances. Repeat to make 36 blocks total.

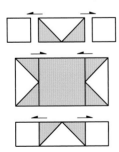
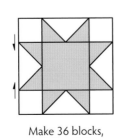

Make 36 blocks,
6½" × 6½".

ASSEMBLING THE QUILT TOP

Referring to the quilt assembly diagram below, lay out the blocks and white 6½" squares in nine rows of seven pieces each, alternating blocks and squares. Join the pieces in each row, then join the rows. The quilt center should measure 42½" × 54½", including seam allowances.

Quilt assembly

ASSEMBLING THE BORDERS

1. Trim the selvages from the five white 2⅜" × 42" strips. Sew the strips together end to end to make one long strip. From this strip, cut two pieces, 42½" long, and two pieces, 58¼" long.

2. Sew three blue gingham and three white 1¼" × 42" strips together as shown to make a strip set. Make three. Cut 96 segments, 1¼" wide.

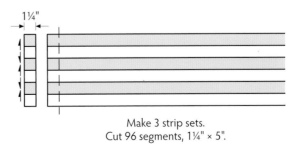

1¼"

Make 3 strip sets.
Cut 96 segments, 1¼" × 5".

3. Sew 11 segments together, and then unstitch the seam where indicated to make a top/bottom pieced border. Repeat to make a total of four identical borders.

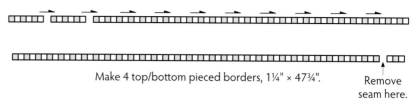

Make 4 top/bottom pieced borders, 1¼" × 47¾". Remove seam here.

4. Sew 13 segments together, and then unstitch the seam where indicated to make an inner side pieced border. Repeat to make two identical borders.

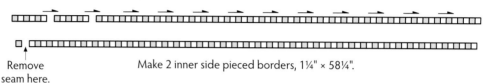

Remove seam here. Make 2 inner side pieced borders, 1¼" × 58¼".

5. Sew 14 segments together, and then unstitch the seam where indicated to make an outer side pieced border. Repeat to make two identical borders.

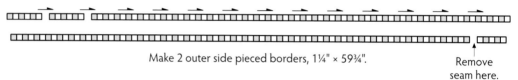

Make 2 outer side pieced borders, 1¼" × 59¾". Remove seam here.

6. Trim the selvages from the six white 3" × 42" strips. Sew the strips together end to end to make one long strip. From this long strip, cut two pieces, 59¾" long, and two pieces, 47¾" long.

7. Trim the selvages from the six white 4" × 42" strips. Sew the strips together end to end to make one long strip. From this long strip, cut two pieces, 59¾" long, and two pieces, 47¾" long.

8. Sew together one white 3" × 59¾" strip, one outer side pieced border, and one white 4" × 59¾" strip as shown to make a side border unit. Make two.

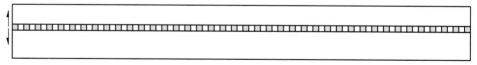

Make 2 side border units, 7¼" × 59¾".

9. Sew together one white 3" × 47¾" strip, one top/bottom pieced border, and one white 4" × 47¾" strip as shown to make the top/bottom border unit. Make two.

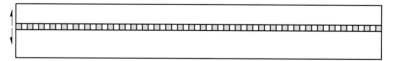

Make 2 top/bottom border units, 7¼" × 47¾".

3. Sew the side border units to the sides of the quilt top, being careful to place the 4"-wide white strip toward the outside of the quilt.

4. Referring to the diagram below, sew star units to both ends of each top/bottom border unit. Then sew these pieced units to the top and bottom edges of the quilt to complete the quilt top.

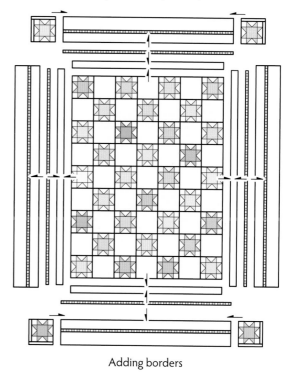

Adding borders

10. Sew a white 1¼" × 6½" strip to the left edge of *each* remaining block. Sew a white 1¼" × 7¼" strip to the *top* of two blocks and to the *bottom* of two different blocks. Each star unit should be 7¼" square, including seam allowances.

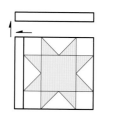

Make 2 of each unit, 7¼" × 7¼".

ADDING THE BORDERS

1. Sew white 2⅜" × 42½" strips to the top and bottom edges of the quilt center. Then sew white 2⅜" × 58¼" strips to the sides.

2. Sew the inner side pieced borders to the sides of the quilt top. Then sew the remaining top/bottom pieced borders to the top and bottom of the quilt top.

FINISHING THE QUILT

For more details on any finishing steps, visit ShopMartingale.com/HowtoQuilt for free, downloadable information.

1. Layer the backing, batting, and quilt top; baste the layers together.

2. Quilt by hand or machine. The quilt shown is machine quilted with an overall echoed-loop design.

3. Use the light blue 2½"-wide strips to make binding, and then attach the binding to the quilt.

A Cuppa

MATERIALS

Yardage is based on 42"-wide fabric.

- 42 squares, 10" × 10", of assorted prints for appliqués*
- 1½ yards of white check for block backgrounds
- 1 yard of off-white solid for block backgrounds and appliqués
- ⅝ yard of ivory solid for block backgrounds
- ⅓ yard of dark pink stripe for inner border
- 1⅞ yards of blue floral for outer border
- ⅝ yard of blue stripe for binding
- 4½ yards of fabric for backing**
- 80" × 80" square of batting
- 1½ yards of lightweight fusible web, such as Steam-a-Seam Lite
- Embroidery floss (optional): warm gray

*A Moda Layer Cake works well, as long as it has 42 squares. You could also use 81 charm squares, 5" × 5", which is two or three charm packs.

**Or 2¼ yards of 80"-wide fabric.

Whether your favorite "cuppa" is coffee, tea, a latté, or a mocha, this fun design celebrates the time we take to enjoy a cup with friends or family, as well as those precious, quiet moments spent savoring a favorite beverage. Choose from two sweet options: a throw-size quilt or a smaller wall hanging.

QUILT SIZE: 72" × 72"
BLOCK SIZE: 6" × 6"

Designed and appliquéd by Brenda Riddle; quilted by Karolyn "Nubin" Jensen

CUTTING

All measurements include ¼" seam allowances.

From the white check, cut:
7 strips, 6½" × 42"; crosscut into 40 squares,
    6½" × 6½"

From the off-white solid, cut:
5 strips, 6½" × 42"; crosscut into 25 squares,
    6½" × 6½"

From the ivory solid, cut:
3 strips, 6½" × 42"; crosscut into 16 squares,
    6½" × 6½"

From the dark pink stripe, cut:
6 strips, 1½" × 42"

From the blue floral, cut:
7 strips, 8¼" × 42"

From the blue stripe, cut:
8 strips, 2½" × 42"

MAKING THE BLOCKS

1. Use the patterns on page 79 to trace small cups, large cups, plates, and plate centers onto fusible web the number of times indicated on each pattern. Leave ½" between tracings.

2. Following the instructions for "Fusible Appliqué" on page 94, press each cup and plate fusible-web shape onto the wrong side of the assorted 10" squares as desired. Press the plate center fusible-web shapes onto the wrong side of off-white solid scraps. Cut out each fabric shape on the drawn line. Peel off the paper backing.

3. Referring to the block appliqué layouts below, center the appliqués on white check, off-white solid, or ivory solid 6½" squares and fuse in place following the manufacturer's instructions. Using thread to match the appliqués and a small blanket stitch, machine sew around each appliqué to make 81 appliquéd blocks.

Make 24
white large
cup blocks.

Make 12
ivory large
cup blocks.

Make 1
white small
cup block.

Make 39
off-white small
cup blocks.

Make 1
off-white
plate block.

Make 4
ivory
plate blocks.

Embroidery Extras

When I was making A Cuppa, I added embroidery to a few of the appliquéd cups—a teabag, curls of steam, and some whipped cream. (I do love a good mocha!) If you'd like to do the same, add the embroidery after stitching the appliqué.

ASSEMBLING THE QUILT TOP

Press all seam allowances as indicated by the arrows.

Lay out the appliquéd blocks in nine rows of nine blocks each. I created a subtle gingham design in the quilt top by alternating the three different background fabrics in each row and from row to row. Refer to the layout diagram below if you'd like to do the same, or create your own fun, scrappy layout. Join the blocks in each row, then join the rows to make the quilt top, which should measure 54½" square, including seam allowances.

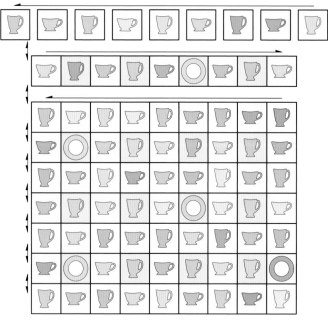

Quilt assembly

ADDING THE BORDERS

1. Sew the dark pink 1½" × 42" strips together end to end. From this long strip, cut two strips, 56½", and two strips, 54½". Sew the 54½"-long strips to opposite sides of the quilt center, then sew the 56½"-long strips to the top and bottom edges of the quilt center. Press the seam allowances toward the inner border.

2. Sew the blue floral 8¼" × 42" strips together end to end. From this long strip, cut two strips, 72", and two strips, 56½". Sew the 56½"-long strips to opposite sides of the quilt center, then sew the 72"-long strips to the top and bottom edges of the quilt center. Press the seam allowances toward the outer border.

FINISHING THE QUILT

For more details on any finishing steps, visit ShopMartingale.com/HowtoQuilt for free, downloadable information.

1. Layer the backing, batting, and quilt top; baste the layers together.

2. Quilt by hand or machine. The quilt shown is machine quilted with a small free-form feather design in the background and a larger free-form feather design in the border.

3. Use the blue stripe 2½"-wide strips to make binding, and then attach the binding to the quilt.

Small cup
Large quilt: Cut 40 from assorted prints.
Small quilt: Cut 20 from assorted prints.

Large cup
Large quilt: Cut 36 from assorted prints.

Plate
Large quilt: Cut 5 from assorted prints.

Plate center
Large quilt: Cut 5 from off-white solid.

Designed and appliquéd by Brenda Riddle; quilted by Karolyn "Nubin" Jensen

Small Cuppa

I have a small but treasured collection of teacups that includes teacups my grandma collected and that my mom then added to. Small Cuppa honors that collection and is the perfect size for a gift or for enhancing a space set for afternoon tea.

QUILT SIZE: 30½" × 36½"
BLOCK SIZE: 6" × 6"

MATERIALS

Yardage is based on 42"-wide fabric.

- 20 squares, 5" × 5", of assorted prints for appliqués*
- 1¼ yard of ivory tone on tone for block backgrounds and borders
- ⅛ yard of blue stripe for middle border
- ⅓ yard of blue gingham for binding
- 1 yard of fabric for backing
- 35" × 41" piece of batting
- ½ yard of lightweight fusible web, such as Steam-a-Seam Lite

*A charm pack works well.

CUTTING

All measurements include ¼" seam allowances.

From the ivory tone on tone, cut:
4 strips, 6½" × 42"; crosscut into 20 squares, 6½" × 6½"
4 strips, 2" × 42"; crosscut into:
    2 strips, 2" × 33½"
    2 strips, 2" × 30½"
4 strips, 1½" × 42"; crosscut into:
    2 strips, 1½" × 30½"
    2 strips, 1½" × 26½"

From the blue stripe, cut:
4 strips, 1" × 42"; crosscut into:
    2 strips, 1" × 32½"
    2 strips, 1" × 27½"

From the blue gingham, cut:
4 strips, 2" × 42"

MAKING THE BLOCKS

1. Use the patterns on page 79 to trace 20 small cups onto fusible web, leaving ½" between tracings.

2. Following the instructions for "Fusible Appliqué" on page 94, press each fusible-web shape onto the wrong side of the assorted 5" squares as desired. Cut out each fabric shape on the drawn line. Peel off the paper backing.

3. Referring to the block appliqué layout below, center the appliqués on ivory 6½" squares and fuse in place following the manufacturer's instructions. Using thread to match the appliqués and a small blanket stitch, machine sew around each appliqué to make 20 blocks.

Make 20
small cup blocks.

ASSEMBLING THE QUILT TOP

Press all seam allowances as indicated by the arrows.

Lay out the appliquéd blocks in five rows of four blocks each. Sew together the blocks in each row. Join the rows to make the quilt top, which should measure 24½" × 30½", including seam allowances.

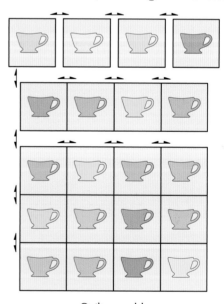

Quilt assembly

ADDING THE BORDERS

1. Sew the ivory 1½" × 30½" strips to opposite sides of the quilt center. Sew the ivory 1½" × 26½" strips to the top and bottom edges of the quilt center.

2. Sew the blue stripe 1" × 32½" strips to opposite sides of the quilt center. Sew the blue stripe 1" × 27½" strips to the top and bottom edges of the quilt center.

3. Sew the ivory 2" × 33½" strips to opposite sides of the quilt center. Sew the ivory 2" × 30½" strips to the top and bottom edges of the quilt center.

FINISHING THE QUILT

For more details on any finishing steps, visit ShopMartingale.com/HowtoQuilt for free, downloadable information.

1. Layer the backing, batting, and quilt top; baste the layers together.

2. Quilt by hand or machine. The quilt shown is machine quilted with an allover leaf design in the background only, leaving the appliqués unquilted.

3. Use the blue gingham 2"-wide strips to make binding, and then attach the binding to the quilt.

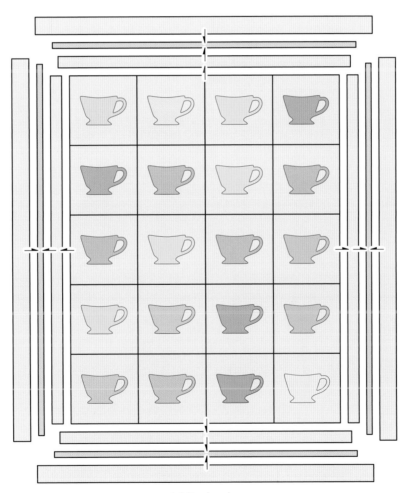

Adding borders

Stepping Stones

Featuring my favorite block—a humble Nine Patch—Stepping Stones is a classic, simple-to-make quilt design. The sample here is made with soft colors, but it would also be gorgeous with a dark background or made with an array of richly colored reproduction prints.

QUILT SIZE: 26" × 26"
BLOCK SIZE: 2¼" × 2¼"

MATERIALS

Yardage is based on 42"-wide fabric.

- ⅜ yard of pink gingham for blocks and binding
- ⅞ yard of white tone on tone for blocks, setting squares, and border
- ⅓ yard of light green print for blocks
- ⅞ yard of fabric for backing
- 30" × 30" square of batting

CUTTING

All measurements include ¼" seam allowances.

From the pink gingham, cut:
3 strips, 2½" × 42"
3 strips, 1¼" × 42"

From the white tone on tone, cut:
3 strips, 3⅛" × 42"
2 strips, 2¾" × 42"; crosscut into 28 squares, 2¾" × 2¾"
9 strips, 1¼" × 42"; crosscut 1 of the strips into 2 strips, 1¼" × 15"

From the light green print, cut:
8 strips, 1¼" × 42"; crosscut 1 of the strips into 1 strip, 1¼" × 15"

MAKING THE BLOCKS

Press all seam allowances as indicated by the arrows.

1. Join one pink and two white 1¼" × 42" strips lengthwise as shown. From this strip set, cut 26 A segments, each 1¼" wide.

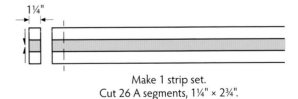

1¼"

Make 1 strip set.
Cut 26 A segments, 1¼" × 2¾".

Designed, pieced, and quilted by Brenda Riddle

2. Join one white and two pink 1¼" × 42" strips lengthwise as shown. From this strip set, cut 13 B segments, each 1¼" wide.

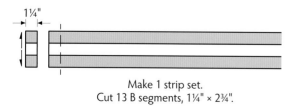

Make 1 strip set.
Cut 13 B segments, 1¼" × 2¾".

3. Join two A segments and one B segment to make a pink Nine Patch block, which should measure 2¾" square, including seam allowances. Repeat to make 13 pink blocks.

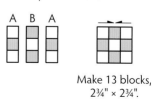

Make 13 blocks,
2¾" × 2¾".

4. Join one white and two green 1¼" × 42" strips lengthwise as shown. Make three strip sets. From these strip sets, cut 80 C segments, each 1¼" wide.

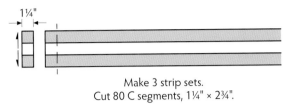

Make 3 strip sets.
Cut 80 C segments, 1¼" × 2¾".

5. Join one green and two white 1¼" × 42" strips lengthwise as shown. Make a second strip set from one green and two white 1¼" × 15" strips. From these strip sets, cut 40 D segments, each 1¼" wide.

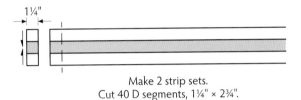

Make 2 strip sets.
Cut 40 D segments, 1¼" × 2¾".

6. Sew together two C segments and one D segment to make a green Nine Patch block, which should measure 2¾" square, including seam allowances. Repeat to make 40 green blocks.

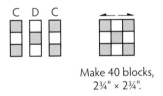

Make 40 blocks,
2¾" × 2¾".

ASSEMBLING THE QUILT TOP

1. To make row 1, sew together five green blocks and four white 2¾" squares as shown. Repeat to make four of row 1.

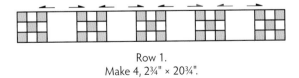

Row 1.
Make 4, 2¾" × 20¾".

2. To make row 2, sew together three pink blocks, four green blocks, and two white 2¾" squares as shown. Repeat to make three of row 2.

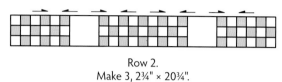

Row 2.
Make 3, 2¾" × 20¾".

3. To make row 3, sew together three white 2¾" squares, four green blocks, and two pink blocks. Repeat to make two of row 3.

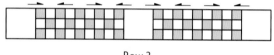

Row 3.
Make 2, 2¾" × 20¾".

4. Join the rows, following the quilt diagram below. The quilt center should measure 20¾" square, including seam allowances.

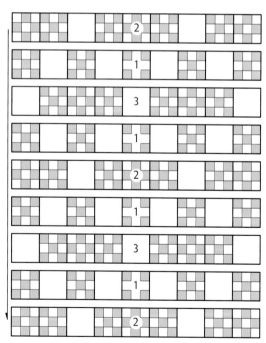

Quilt assembly

ADDING THE BORDER

Trim the selvages off the three white 3⅛" × 42" strips and sew them together end to end. From this long strip, cut two lengths, 20¾", and two lengths, 26". Sew the 20¾" lengths to opposite sides of the quilt center. Sew the 26" lengths to the top and bottom edges.

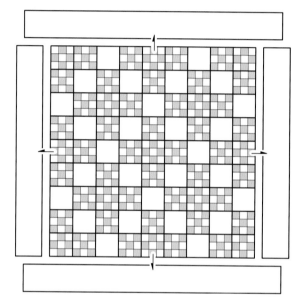

Adding the border

FINISHING THE QUILT

For more details on any finishing steps, visit ShopMartingale.com/HowtoQuilt for free, downloadable information.

1. Layer the backing, batting, and quilt top; baste the layers together.

2. Quilt by hand or machine. The quilt shown is machine quilted with an allover design of spirals and feathers.

3. Use the pink gingham 2½"-wide strips to make binding, and then attach the binding to the quilt.

Mills' Cabin

You'll notice that the quilt layout has five dark Star blocks (with light borders) and four light Star blocks (with dark borders), placed so that once assembled, a larger star appears! The scrappy Star blocks contain what I call "little butterfly" four-patch units, with an outer half-square-triangle border.

QUILT SIZE: 17" × 17"
BLOCK SIZE: 5½" × 5½"

MATERIALS

Yardage is based on 42"-wide fabric.

- 23 squares, 5" × 5", of assorted light prints for blocks*
- 23 squares, 5" × 5", of assorted dark prints for blocks*
- ⅛ yard of gray stripe for binding
- ⅝ yard of fabric for backing
- 21" × 21" square of batting

Two charm packs should provide enough light and dark squares. If you purchase charm packs, you may have enough remaining squares to make a pieced backing, if desired.

CUTTING

All measurements include ¼" seam allowances.

From the assorted light print squares, cut:
10 squares, 3⅝" × 3⅝"; cut the squares in half diagonally to make 20 triangles
36 squares, 2" × 2"
32 squares, 1½" × 1½"

From the assorted dark print squares, cut:
8 squares, 3⅝" × 3⅝"; cut the squares in half diagonally to make 16 triangles
36 squares, 2" × 2"
40 squares, 1½" × 1½"

From the gray stripe, cut:
2 strips, 2" × 42"

MAKING THE BLOCKS

Press all seam allowances as indicated by the arrows.

1. Draw a diagonal line from corner to corner on the back of each light 2" square.

2. Place a light 2" square on top of a dark 2" square, right sides together, and sew ¼" from each side of the diagonal line as shown. Cut along the drawn diagonal line, press, and trim to 1½" square. Repeat to make 72 half-square-triangle units.

Make 72 units.

3. To make a light four-patch unit, sew together two half-square-triangle units and two light 1½" squares as shown. The unit should measure 2½" square, including seam allowances. Repeat to make 16 light four-patch units.

Make 16 units,
2½" × 2½".

4. Using half-square-triangle units and dark 1½" squares, repeat step 3 to make 20 dark four-patch units.

Make 20 units,
2½" × 2½".

5. To make a light star unit, sew together four light four-patch units as shown. The star unit should measure 4½" square, including seam allowances. Repeat to make four light star units.

Make 4 units,
4½" × 4½".

6. Using dark four-patch units, repeat step 5 to make five dark star units.

Make 5 units,
4½" × 4½".

7. For ease in placement, fold each light and dark triangle in half and make a slight crease to mark the center of the triangle.

8. Center and sew a dark triangle to each side of a light star; be careful when handling the bias edges of the triangles since they can easily stretch out of shape. The block should measure 6" square, including seam allowances. Repeat to make four dark blocks.

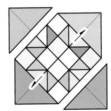 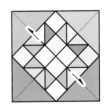

Make 4 dark blocks,
6" × 6".

9. Using light triangles and dark stars, repeat step 8 to make five light blocks.

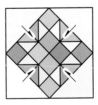

Make 5 light blocks,
6" × 6".

Designed, pieced, and quilted by Brenda Riddle

ASSEMBLING THE QUILT TOP

Lay out the light and dark blocks in three rows, alternating light and dark blocks. Join the blocks in each row, then join the rows to make the quilt top.

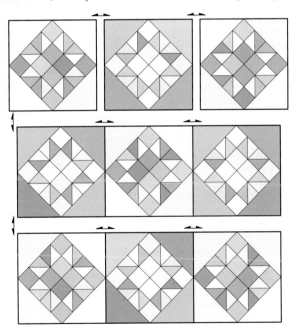

Quilt assembly

FINISHING THE QUILT

For more details on any finishing steps, visit ShopMartingale.com/HowtoQuilt for free, downloadable information.

1. Layer the backing, batting, and quilt top; baste the layers together.

2. Quilt by hand or machine. The quilt shown is machine quilted with allover stippling.

3. Use the gray stripe 2"-wide strips to make binding, and then attach the binding to the quilt.

Special Techniques

Here are some of the techniques that I used to make the projects in this book.

FUSIBLE APPLIQUÉ

While you can use whatever method of appliqué you prefer, I used fusible appliqué for the quilts in this book. I like to use the lightest-weight fusible web I can find, such as Steam-a-Seam Lite or Pellon Lightweight Wonder-Under. I stitch a very small machine blanket stitch around the shapes, and after washing, I don't think anyone can tell that the appliqués were fused.

Here are some general directions for using fusible web, but be sure to follow the manufacturer's directions for the type of fusible you use.

1. Trace the appliqué shapes onto the paper side of the fusible web. Leave ½" between shapes. If you're having trouble seeing to trace, use a light box or sunlit window.

2. Cut out the shapes, leaving ⅛" to ¼" around each shape.

3. Use an iron to press the appliqué shapes onto the *wrong* side of the fabric.

4. Cut out the shapes exactly on the drawn lines.

5. Peel off the paper backing, lay out the shapes on the background fabric, and press. Allow the shapes to cool.

6. Blanket-stitch the appliqué pieces to the background. I like to use 50-weight thread in a coordinating color.

Use a Pressing Sheet

I like to use an appliqué pressing sheet when pressing my appliqués onto the background fabric. A pressing sheet is a double-sided, multipurpose craft sheet made from high-temperature glass coated with a nonstick surface. For fusing appliqués, place the appliqué layout under the pressing sheet, arrange all the overlapping pieces on top of the pressing sheet, and carefully press all the shapes with your iron. After cooling, the entire design can be gently peeled off the pressing sheet and placed onto the background fabric.

EMBROIDERY STITCHES

Backstitch

Chain stitch

Colonial knot

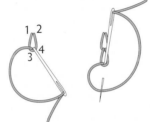

French knot
(2 wraps)

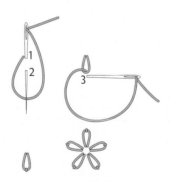

Lazy daisy stitch

Satin stitch

Stem stitch

About the Author

BRENDA RIDDLE, the creative force behind Acorn Quilt & Gift Company, knows that "great oaks from little acorns grow." What does that mean for quiltmakers? As Brenda likes to say, "If you see a design that you love or a pattern that inspires you, but you doubt your ability, remember that all it takes is one step at a time." We all can grow our little acorns of inspiration into handcrafted pieces to treasure now and for years to come.

After a professional life centered on interior design and the architectural field, Brenda put her skills to work teaching art and design to high school students. Switching gears to indulge her love of sewing, Brenda launched Acorn Quilt & Gift Company, creating and selling patterns for quilts. Later she expanded to add embroidery, counted cross-stitch, and punchneedle patterns under the umbrella of Brenda Riddle Designs. A longtime fabric designer for Moda, she enjoys coming up with new fabric collections that exhibit her trademark vintage feel—and putting those fabrics to use in beautiful quilts.

Brenda calls Arizona home, where she lives with her dad and her dog, Bailey.